D1205030

Using Drama to Bring Language to Life

Ideas, Games and Activities for Teachers of Languages and Language Arts

Sheila Robbie
Writer/Researcher

Tina Ruggirello
University of Windsor

Bernie Warren
University of Windsor

Captus Press

PROPERTY OF
Baker College Allen Park

USING DRAMA TO BRING LANGUAGE TO LIFE:
IDEAS, GAMES AND ACTIVITIES FOR TEACHERS OF
LANGUAGES AND LANGUAGE ARTS

Copyright © 2001 by Sheila Robbie, Tina Ruggirello,
Bernie Warren and Captus Press Inc.

All rights reserved. No part of this book may be reproduced,
stored in a retrieval system, or transmitted, in any form or by
any means, electronic, mechanical, photocopying, recording, or
otherwise, without prior written permission of the copyright
holders. Correspondence can be sent to Captus Press Inc.

Captus Press Inc.
York University Campus, 4700 Keele Street,
North York, Ontario   M3J 1P3   Canada
Telephone: (416) 736–5537   Fax: (416) 736–5793
Email: info@captus.com   Internet: www.captus.com

Cover design and artwork: John Settels (www.johnsettels.com)

Canadian Cataloguing in Publication Data
Robbie, Sheila, 1960–
    Using drama to bring language to life : ideas, games and
activities for teachers of languages and language arts

Includes bibliographical references and index.
ISBN 1-55322-005-6

1. Language and languages — Study and teaching.
2. Drama in education.
I. Ruggirello, Tina, 1962– . II. Warren, Bernie, 1953– . III. Title.

P53.297.R62 2001   407'.1   C00-933043-7

Canada ┃•┃ We acknowledge the financial support of the
Government of Canada through the Book
Publishing Industry Development Program (BPIDP) for our
publishing activities.

0 9 8 7 6 5 4 3 2 1
Printed in Canada

Contents

*To our mentors, our colleagues,
our students and our families.*

FOREWORD

Using Drama to Bring Language to Life reminds me of the human seriousness of play. In his book *From Ritual to Theatre*, Victor Turner (1982) writes about the liberating capacities of the creative that combine the cognitive, the affective, and the volitional within the context of normative constraints. Robbie, Ruggirello, and Warren understand the importance of in(ter)ventions in the classroom. They have coupled properties that stimulate knowledge and discovery with motivational "gaming". Their work is truly a process approach whereby learning occurs through experience. Their *Ideas, Games and Activities for Teachers of Languages and Language Arts* are more than instructive tools; they are moments in which the critical and the creative are interwoven in action and interaction.

Teachers will immediately recognize the co-evolving worlds of drama and language study. Not only do the activities in this book bring language to life, they also reinforce the living world on stage in which the everyday is meaningfully recast and performed.

The teaching ideas in *Using Drama* will help teachers pose difficult questions with their students, exposing the ways in which power circulates and how social agency can mediate relationship in ritualized spaces. Moreover, they will assist teachers in the role-play of conflict resolution through the clarification, re-enaction, and reconstruction of dramatic situations. The power of this text is that it not only provides language learning opportunities in world-like situations, it also promotes the kind of reflection that lasts long after the drama ends, the kind that can, indeed, promote growth and understanding.

Robbie, Ruggirello, and Warren provide careful instruction of various theatrical techniques to assist students and teachers throughout the stages from enrollment in dramatic role-play experiences to serious contemplation and critique. There are also suggestions for observation and analysis as student performers grow in confidence. The journey from idea to stage will occur rapidly with the practical assistance provided in this text, making school a place of play(ing)/ learning.

Using Drama especially challenges the educational system to reconsider the interplay between teacher, learner, and context. Knowledge in action is a reconsidered relationship between mind and body. Moreover, the pedagogical significance of play in language study emphasizes the shifting, embodied context of meaning.

— Diane DuBose Brunner
Professor of English
Michigan State University

ACKNOWLEDGEMENTS

I (SR) am indebted to Tony Burgess, Gunther Kress, James Brooker, Anton Franks and Sue Hubbert who each played an important part in the initial research and practice behind this book; to my students and colleagues around the world who have helped me criticize and crystallize my ideas; and to my husband John for his patience, creativity and intellectual curiosity: Thank you everyone for making this journey possible.

I (TR) am grateful to my co-authors for their influence, knowledge and inspiration; to Sue Ann Martin for launching my journey and for continuing to inspire and influence from afar. To my students, past and present and future for challenging me to critically examine my own work and to my husband and family for their continued support.

I (BW) want to thank Bert Amies, Caroline Simonds, George Mager, Keith Yon, Richard Courtney, David Booth and Jinny Koste, each of whom have been both mentors and colleagues to me, and through their love of what they do have served as inspiration for my work. And of course my family Julie and Alora, without whom my contributions to this book would not have occurred.

INTRODUCTION

I . I WHAT THIS BOOK IS ABOUT

Everyone seems to be walking past our classroom today. They would wouldn't they? Just when it is the one with all the windows facing the courtyard. Heads move surreptitiously in our direction. When I turn I sense the eyes peering in, scorching holes in my back.

"Move out of the way, Miss says ALL the desks have to be moved," screams Luis.

Clatter, bump, scratch. I wonder what I have started. I wonder where it will end? (Little did I know...) I had been up most of the night going over the session. Awake most of the rest wondering if I had done the right thing. Momentarily, in situ, I let a brief hesitation flicker through my mind, then disappear. Nothing ventured, nothing gained. I take a deep breath and step right forward:

— Gather round everyone...

Eighteen years later I bless that first day I used drama in the classroom, with all its inconsistencies and hiccoughs, its laughter, its tears. Since that time drama as a teaching method and a subject has been and is continually evolving and hopefully will always do so. Second and foreign language theories have taken enormous leaps and bounds, particularly in the last two decades and are now adapting to the different types of classroom and new technologies that form an integral part of our lives today. In the midst of this, drama still lives on.

This book reflects the authors' belief that working in the drama medium, in meaningful contexts, enriches and improves the language learning process and empowers students with the confidence, motivation and enthusiasm to do their very best. As practitioners and researchers from different disciplines and cultures we

I

bring together countless experiences in numerous fields of expertise.

This book is the result of working together and with one another's students (average ages 5–65) in different parts of the world; of working with students and teachers of different nationalities respectively learning and teaching different languages (second languages, foreign languages, mother tongue); with drama students and teachers, who use their talents in the language classroom and with language arts teachers; and, of extensive research in mother and second/foreign tongues.

As its title suggests, *Using Drama to Bring Language to Life: Ideas, Games and Activities for Teachers of Languages and Language Arts* provides a broad range of ideas and strategies that are designed to help enliven the learning of languages and develop students' general language abilities. It is primarily intended as a resource for teachers of second and foreign languages. However many of the ideas presented here work equally well with students studying their first/native language. As such, this book will also be helpful to ANY teacher looking for ideas for their Language, Language Arts or Drama classes.

The material in this book is presented in an accessible way so that all teachers, from novices to seasoned veterans, may draw from it at their own level of expertise and use it in accordance with their particular classroom. Specifically designed templates take you through different **drama sessions** in which the **target language** is an instrument rather than a subject; a means through which meanings are discussed, pondered and made rather than the focus of attention. The sessions have been selected to illustrate the various ways in which drama can be used and to provide maximum flexibility for both student and teacher. To this end, suggestions are made as to how material can be adapted to different groups and how teachers unfamiliar with a dramatic approach to language learning may get the most from the ideas presented.

We believe that when used in this way, drama for language learning not only provides a whole learning experience but brings language learning to life.

1.2 DRAMA AS A LEARNING MEDIUM

Drama for language learning is about working exclusively in the **target language**, about fictional role-taking, improvisation and real communication. Extensive research and experience have taught us that one of the great powers of drama is that taking the emphasis away from language (and putting it on imagination, the making of meaning/s in order to solve dramatic "problems") actually leads to language improvement. The idea is that students learn about language by working in it and with it, individually and in groups.

In the day to day classroom often students are focussed on language as the object of study, an emphasis on correct use and usage and a desire to please the teacher. In the drama classroom, the aim is to get the students so involved in the action and the outcome of future actions that although they focus on what they say and how they say it, they see this as a means to an end rather than a test. In a drama session in which students are fully involved and in which the teacher does not overtly correct language, we have found that students actually strive harder than usual to communicate than in a more usual classroom situation. In the absence of given set phrases they are also forced to either individually or collectively come up with some way of conveying what it is they need to convey. Language spoken or written with conviction and with a true purpose and audience is the type of language teachers are always looking for.

Thus when students begin a drama session a balance needs to be struck between enforcing the **target language (TL)** rule (not allowing them to communicate in anything except the **target language**) and in getting them so involved in the action that they are no longer conscious of being in a language classroom.

Drama also makes language learning part of a broader picture, that of everyday life. Different possibilities, different ways of seeing the situation enter the classroom. The age-old argument of giving a student a safe arena in which to work does bear fruit: an atmosphere of confidence and encouragement can be productive. With rivalry between peers removed, richer and fuller language results as nervousness is less of an issue. Indeed our research and practice has shown that this way of working leads to improved student response, expression, communication and writing.

Drama facilitates spontaneous learning in an environment that is as authentic, natural and contextualized as possible. Students therefore are not learning by memorizing, or repeating set phrases in contrived situations but by using language as a cognitive instrument while discovering the way words and their meanings are used in the **target language**. Consequently, when drama is introduced into the language arena it becomes important to speak not of language acquisition but of language *learning* and *development*. This means that the **target language** and/or its component parts are not seen as something that the student has or has not "done". The material in this book therefore works with what the student already knows, in a different context, building upon both this and the day-to-day work of the practitioner in the language classroom. It is intended to be used alongside and interact with your other language activities.

What often comes of surprise to newcomers to drama is both the amount and the numerous types of language that can be involved in any ONE **drama session**. To name a few:

- analyzing, discussing;
- organizing, selecting, sequencing, comparing;
- informing, reporting;
- presenting an argument, convincing, negotiating;
- questioning, interviewing, answering;
- accusing, denying, defending, explaining;
- writing (in many forms);
- reading.

Teachers will find that, by using these in meaningful contexts, students pick up new structures, words and expressions without really noticing — as they hear their peers speak and read, etc. Indeed, in the need to become understood, they even find expressions they did not know they knew. Drama is also very good at highlighting problem areas in grammar which you can note and cover in subsequent language lessons. Teachers interested in this should refer to the at a glance guide to languages as well as the table of language abilities found at the end of each template.

To summarize, the aim is to use several dramatic processes with different focuses within the **target language** to:

- shift the emphasis away from language itself to the meanings behind it;
- make language learning student centred and meaning centred rather than grammatically controlled;
- solicit both personal expression and group negotiation;
- make language learning fun;
- provide material for further language/drama activities which continue the language learning.

In the process, students learn about:

- language in context: namely how certain choices affect the message (intonation, nuances, appropriateness, register, etc.);
- word meanings — which change and evolve;
- fluency, both spoken and written (as opposed to the stringing together of grammatical phrases);
- the way concepts change from one language to another.

This is important, as knowledge of the language system is indispensable but will get us only so far. We also bring to any kind of text everything pertinent that we know about the culture whose language we are speaking. Drama helps students access that knowledge and the writing afterwards consolidates the learning.

The value of writing exercises as a continuation of the drama session cannot be overemphasized. The interest generated by the drama carries over into the writing, involving a constant dialogue between the action of the drama, student imagination and language ability. Writing of this kind not only teaches about ambiguities, it also provides an opportunity to think about them and express personal views. As a result, students pay particular attention to expression.

The writing/drama relationship:

- involves the student taking a particular stance as a writer. The writing is infused with who the student is and what they are writing about. Gone are sentences written to fill the page which say nothing;
- doesn't teach sub-skills. Instead, students find out for themselves how written language functions. They not only learn the system but also how to make use of it;
- can be designed to practise or develop language matters which have arisen during the session.

Be forewarned — drama is not a magic wand which once waved produces students fluent in the **target language**. However, when properly designed, it can and does bring exciting results, not only in oral but also in grammatical, syntactical and written abilities.

This book will call on you to read and think critically about a variety of lesson templates which have worked for us, to challenge your preconceptions of dramatic role-play as the taking of set roles for the practice of certain grammatical structures "at the railway station" for example. We invite you to taste our own special recipe of drama and language learning.

Working in this way is not always easy. It may require some creative reorganizing in order to work in spaces and time frames that are non-negotiable. However, it does:

- encourage student/teacher interaction: through talk, and play;
- build upon student interest/agency: -students are drawn into the dramatic context that is being explored; they develop a personal connection to the work as it unfolds;
- work towards goals: all participants (students and teacher) work together for a common purpose;
- lead to appreciation of individual strengths and needs: there is something to gain for each participant, regardless of their level of achievement.;
- provide rich language material to work with in the way you ascertain most useful for your particular classroom.

It was the end-of-term staff meeting and we were discussing both student results and attitude.

"How do you get your students to be so enthusiastic?" asked one.

"How come their test results have improved so drastically when you have been spending so much classroom time on this drama thing?" inquired another.

I could but smile inwardly. I began: — Well you see this drama thing ...

I.3 HOW THE BOOK IS STRUCTURED

As with the first of this series, *Drama Games*, this book is intended as a practical introduction, the beginning of a story, which each practitioner will continue and develop in their own way.

We have devised a presentation system in the form of templates of different types of lesson/**drama session** which have worked for the authors. In the appendices teachers will find additional material to use in the templates such as stories, articles, songs, poems etc.

The book is a resource book full of different 'recipes' which have been tried, tasted and proven to work. Yet like any recipe in any book they can be changed and altered with different ingredients (different teachers, different students, different goals, different educational environments). Within this book you will find suggestions and examples of how activities in the templates can be adapted to suit different classrooms.

However, this is a handbook for teachers to dip in and choose from, it is not a book to be followed chronologically from one page to the next. The templates are organized in order of ease and complexity. We would suggest that teachers unfamiliar with drama start with those at the beginning of each section, until they become familiar with this way of working. Each practitioner will bring something different and worthwhile to the experience. Therefore, with time, we encourage teachers to mix these methods with their own in order to find their own particular way of working. Indeed, we believe you will benefit most by making your own combinations and using your own criteria for selecting sessions. Perhaps a **drama session** coincides with a particular theme or topic to be covered in their set book, perhaps another appeals to their imagination or engages with a particular type of language that the students need to learn. Teachers interested in these points should refer to the section *At a Glance Guide to Language.*

For simplicity's sake we use the term **target language (TL)** throughout the book to refer to ANY language the student is studying; whether this is the student's second, third or fourth language. Since the activities we present are the same, it allows us as authors to speak to teachers all over the world at the same time; whether you are working as a teacher of ESL, EFL , FFL, mother tongue etc., whether the student knows any other languages apart from their own, and whether or not the language you are teaching is part of your student's culture or immediate surroundings.

In the interest of clarity we have opted for using one gender for the teacher and one for the student. We have used "she" to denote the teacher and "he" to denote the student. Whilst this will be annoying for male teachers we hope you will realize our intentions are merely to make the material simple, clutter-free and grammatically correct as deemed by a book on language learning. The book is divided into the following sections:

PREFACE TO TEMPLATES

This section takes you through the template system, the role of teacher and the educational considerations brought up by working in the drama medium. It also explains how to work with the templates presented. As language classes may not only be filled with different ages and academic abilities but also students from diverse cultural backgrounds, ideas are given as to how to adapt the existing templates to your particular classroom situation. This latter section is links with 6.3 where specific examples are given.

TEMPLATES

These are plans of **drama sessions** and are divided into:
- single sessions: templates which can, in theory, be done in one session;
- drama units: templates which are formed of two or more linked sessions.

We do however emphasize that drama time is *flexi-time*. A teacher may decide to carry part of the drama over to another class period due to the age or language level of the participants, or to extend the theme or language work. Each template suggests ways to further develop each session via writing, projects or drama activities.

PRE-DRAMA ACTIVITIES

These are warm-up games and activities, movement or language based used, as indicated, before a **drama session** to relax students and start them moving.

Group formation exercises

These are fun ways of dividing students into specific-size groups which teachers may like to use where indicated in the template.

At-a-glance Guide to Language

Our language abilities matrix shows the different language points practised in each activity in each template. Teachers may find this of use when selecting a template or going over the language used in the session.

The table of drama topics is of use for teachers who have to teach from a set language book which enforces the teaching of language through set topics. It will help those teachers select a **session** to fit in with their book.

Bibliography

This lists texts for further reading and other source books for ideas.

Appendices

These include sections for use with the templates where indicated, composed of stories, poems, newspaper articles, guided imagery, songs etc., and examples of how templates can be adapted to different classrooms with reference to four specific templates.

Glossary

Due to the cross-disciplinary and cross-cultural nature of our work we have included a glossary of drama terms explaining terminology as used in this book. Specific drama terminology is marked in the text in **bold**. Please take time to refer to the explanations of how we use these terms as many cultural as well as technical and disciplinary nuances apply.

Index

PREFACE TO TEMPLATES

2. I ROLE(S) OF THE TEACHER

In the **drama** environment our role as teachers is different than usual. We have to learn to stand back and let the drama develop. We need to swallow the impulse to correct, and to work in the background. As the helper rather than provider of knowledge, we help:

- facilitate, encourage, guide through sensitive intervention and not to correct language errors;
- prepare the language we wish the students to practise;
- surreptitiously steer the way the language is used, through the fictional process;
- encourage student creation and participation in order to generate meaning;
- maintain the TL rule.

This change in teacher/student relationship does not mean the teacher is out of control:

- when there is a group problem it is easy to intercede in the drama at any time and guide the students towards understanding by
  - ➤ introducing a new turn of the situation **in role**;
  - ➤ introducing stimuli, (a letter, an announcement);
  - ➤ stopping the drama and asking the students to step out of role and discuss their situation;
- you can upgrade language or use incorrect language in a correct manner without students being consciously aware you are doing so in the following ways:
  - ➤ **in role,** repeating something incorrect, correctly as part of the ongoing conversation;
  - ➤ in the **drama circle**, summarizing in your own words what has happened so far;

- when students are working out their drama activities you are always available for each group or individual providing whatever help they need. In this sense it is much easier than in the usual classroom situation to talk to and monitor students individually.

The ground rule for the **drama sessions** is that they are carried out in the **target language**. In special cases, as in those of near beginners and very young children, a little of their native language may be permitted. However, our experience is that drama works best when in the TL. It is natural for students to revert to their native language, when discussing, organizing or preparing drama activities: prompt, insist and you will get results. Students eventually become so involved in the process that they use every means available to them to communicate, and intermediate students no longer realize they are working in a different language.

Curriculum requirements have to be borne in mind. We hope the templates will show how curriculum objectives, such as the learning of certain grammar points, can be met with the help of this method of working. A set language book may be a requirement of your specific institution. Mostly such books are divided into themes/topics such as emigration, fame, power, medicine, the family etc., which lend themselves perfectly to drama. **Drama sessions** can also be used to supplement reading comprehension and grammar work in class, or to work on a topic about which the students are required to write an essay.

All of the authors are experienced in working in this way, but in order for the recipe to work correctly, the strength of the ingredients needs to be known. We cannot know each group as you cannot know each new class when you come to teach them. Thus, you as practitioner need to understand the group and how they grow, tailoring each session to the group's and your own specific needs. In doing so, you should bear in mind:

- drama presupposes that a certain amount of grammar is known:
  - ➢ do not use a session to practise something already covered, but to explore what students know and need to know.
- You should work within your comfort zone:
  - ➢ templates are ordered by level of drama difficulty, so start with the easier first if you are not used to this way of working; later you can adapt templates yourself;
- cultural norms and practices may influence the way students interact or are prepared to "let go";
  - ➢ certain kinds of body language are accepted in one country and not in another. Some students will be used to touching one another, others won't. Some will need more time, per-

haps via pre-rehearsal techniques, to relax and get used to moving about, while others will fall into it naturally.

 ➢ some may be very shy, reticent or show animosity at the beginning. Time usually brings them round.

• drama time is always flexi-time: build your drama around your classroom and do not rush, if necessary extend a session into another class period;

• remember practical considerations — allow time to create space by moving back the desks;

 ➢ don't use a room with a stage or with fixed desks;

 ➢ don't put students in the spotlight;

 ➢ try for a room away from disturbing noise;

 ➢ flexible lighting is an added extra.

Drama places special demands on the students. It will take time for them to value their own judgements, their own ideas and to use their own views and personalities to take the drama forward. And of course, there will be a few "hard cases" who will need to become part of the process to perceive its value. In many cases it helps to have a talk with students prior to their first **drama session**, to emphasise:

• drama in the language classroom is about questioning and reflecting, not performance (drama is not about acting but about being in someone else's skin for a while);

• there are no right answers;

• everything contributed by the participants will be considered;

• language abilities are not on show, the aim is communication not grammatical accuracy (that, teachers will find, comes of its own accord).

It is also important to advise students to wear loose clothing and to tell them drama involves a lot of movement and often a lot of sitting on the floor. Many templates/classes can however be adapted for people who are less agile or less physically able.

Furthermore, the only thing to do is to choose your template, prepare your materials and begin.

2.2 HOW TO CHOOSE A TEMPLATE

Most of the templates are geared to students with intermediate and/or advanced language level abilities; however the first few templates may be used with beginners and get progressively more complex. If you do not have a strong drama background or are not sure where to start, we suggest you may want to begin with the simpler templates. By working through from the simple to the more complex, one by one, you will begin to acquire a level of skill necessary to work with the content of the more complex templates.

As with cookery there are certain ground rules and specific tools which can be used to help along the way. Teachers should check:

- If the template is suitable for your particular class, although in principle all templates can be done by, or adapted for, most students;
- Which language abilities you specifically wish to cover; you should look at the language abilities table (see 8.2) which lists the templates one by one and shows which language abilities are covered in the activities as they are presented. If you then wish to see a particular session in more detail you should look at the table at the end of the template in question, which goes through the template activity by activity;
- The language themes table if you teach via set topics;
- If you have access to all materials needed for the session;
  - ➤ All of us tend to use certain props in **drama sessions** — be they hats, candles, swords or curtain material. In our experience, if students are not used to drama, they often find it helps if they have something to grasp hold of in order to assume a character. It also helps to create something tactile, therefore other tools such as coloured paper, pens, silver foil, glue, scissors, sticky tape are often needed. However we suggest that teachers do not get lost in props and costumes as too much attention in this area can be distracting and take away from the drama work itself.
- If you need to prepare materials from the appendices;
- If you are familiar and at ease with all the drama strategies which may occur during the session (see glossary); do not attempt something too complicated if you are new to this;
- The room you will be teaching in is suitable for drama: desks are moveable, etc.

2.3 HOW TO USE A TEMPLATE

The best way to introduce you to the template system is to take you through the different things that you will find in each template in the order that they appear.

CHECK LIST

There is a check list at the beginning of each template telling you with what type of stimulus the drama begins and the optimal class (although you can usually adapt the template to fit a bigger or smaller class). It will also list things you will need, things you need to prepare and give an indication of your main role in the session.

Pre-Drama Activities

The session starts with a game or exercise to get the students used to moving around the classroom and/or speaking out loud — and to get rid of any nervous energy or giggles.

Teachers may want to spend some time exploring the games and activities in section 6 in order to familiarize themselves and the students with the warm-ups and this way of working. Also see the references in the bibliography for source books for games and activities.

These activities are optional. They are often worth the extra time as they help students to forget about "language as a subject". Teachers should work within their comfort zone and use games and activities the students will find easy and fun. The aim here is not to test but to relax both mind and body. Remember to begin here in the TL and continue through the session.

In a few cases we indicate specific pre-drama activities which are not optional. In this case the teacher will be talked through the activity in the template itself.

Group Formation Exercises

Reference will be made to group formation exercises throughout the template, before activities when students have to work together or where specific-size groups are needed. These are fun ways of forming groups when students have to work together. *These are also optional.* They help in forming random groupings to ensure friends and abilities are mixed around the class. They can also be tailored to promote certain language points the teacher wishes to highlight. In cases however where these exercises would detract from important action developing, or a specific atmosphere that has been created, the teacher should allocate groups and proceed immediately with the drama action.

Stimuli

Each drama session starts with a specific stimulus. An appeal to the imagination, via story, activity, brainstorming, etc., initiates student interaction and arouses their interest. For example you may produce objects and the students will make up a story around them or you may give the beginning of a story, stopping at a suitably provocative or indecisive moment.

ESTABLISHING THEME, FOCUS AND FICTIONAL SITUATION

The theme/focus of the session is established and usually some "problem" is introduced which needs to be solved or worked through.

We tend to use fictional situations which are removed from daily life in our society today, namely we choose to work in a fantasy/storytelling world. Dramas set up around everyday situations in contemporary society, such as problems at home, drug abuse etc., more than often lead to:

• stereotypical portrayals; and/or
• the production of characters that the students think the teacher wants to see or are politically correct.

We find that in a "fantasy" environment students are much more likely to let go and explore different viewpoints and solutions to the problem posed in the session, since they are one further step removed from being themselves, or whoever it is they think the teacher would like them to be. It is always easy subsequently, in further sessions or assignments, to make the points that have been highlighted in drama relate to real life.

DRAMA ACTIVITIES

Unless stated these are not optional. They have been carefully designed and structured for maximum language opportunity, each one is necessary for the building up of the session. It is preferable to finish the **drama session** another day rather than to skip activities in order to finish. Drama takes and needs time in order to work optimally.

A series of drama games, activities and techniques, each with a different focus, are used to work through the theme. Some of these strategies may be familiar to some of you, others will be new. Each strategy is signalled in **bold** in the text and described in the glossary, which we urge you to refer to. Central to the work is:

• fictional role-taking — the assuming of the actions and words of a fictional character whose language, character and actions develop as the drama unfolds;
• **improvisation** — the characters, their reactions and the words they speak are not set beforehand and set phrases are not given;

- interaction — language and subjects interact both physically/socially and mentally/cognitively with all the participants, their personalities, interests or beliefs;
- real communication: finding other ways of doing, other ways of saying for real purposes.

Students work both individually and in groups (for practical as well as pedagogical reasons) towards a collective end and may or may not be asked to share their work with the rest of the class.

Note that not only the activities themselves but their planning should, as far as possible (depending on student ability) be carried out in the **target language**.

The important thing for the drama/language learning relationship is that student interest and agency is maintained. Language becomes part of the learning process, intrinsically linked to the demands imposed by the need to communicate in order to work through the various activities in each workshop.

The teacher's role becomes that of facilitator rather than audience/examiner. As language becomes part of the overall event students are no longer in competition with each other. A group spirit is created and everyone is important in the process, no-one is marginalized.

Instructions for the teacher are indicated in italic.

Teachers should also refer to the sections on adapting activities and templates for specific ideas about how to adapt templates to their particular classroom. Where some activities are specifically geared to one type of student there will also be suggestions regarding possible adaptations for different ages or language ability within the template itself.

ADAPTATIONS

In some of the activities there are indications of how to adapt that particular activity to a different type of classroom. See also our sections on adaptations in the preface and appendices.

CONCLUDING REMARKS

It is important at the end of every template that the teacher congratulates students on how well they have worked in the **target language** and points out interesting parts: I liked it when you ... because...

Post-Drama Activities

The drama continues on paper as students carry out a series of writing activities. Sometimes this writing takes place during or in between some of the dramatic processes in the above section. Usually , due to time restrictions, it is assigned subsequent to a **drama session**, either in class or at home. It is not, we will stress, tacked on as an afterthought. It is to be seen as an ongoing part of the drama, which is why many of the initial writing exercises are **in role**. It is also why we find that postponing oral discussion until writing has taken place adds a wealth of genuine/original response to the drama. We have found that writing after oral discussion of the class is always influenced by what was discussed in class.

Selected writing exercises are listed at the end of each template. These are not rigid. You may like to substitute/adapt activities from other templates, to suit your particular classes, or to add in language items which relate to what students have been doing.

In some cases we have included ways in which we have extended the work beyond one session. With this, we intend to give you ideas rather than set a fixed pattern. Each classroom and each teacher will have a different set of priorities and concerns. Hopefully individual readers will have other suggestions and responses as this type of work (as indeed any drama session), can go in many directions.

We suggest those of you who teach language through a set book based on themes extend the drama by relating it to the theme as presented in your own language book by (1) reference to the book itself or (2) through language or literature exercises based on the theme.

Subsequent to writing activities, there are certain generic activities that you can relate to all of the templates, such as:

- recap on what has been done and write up new vocabulary or expressions on the board;
- ask questions about what has happened in relation to the plot (beginners); in relation to how they felt (intermediate/advanced);
- class develops or retells a story around the class, each person saying a line;
- for **storydrama**: students look at a part of the book and compare it to what has happened in the drama;
- raise possible questions relating to plot;
  - ➤ what if the Prince never found Cinderella? What if Cinderella's foot swelled up and the slipper didn't fit her?;
- class prepares one or a series of scenes to show how the drama story could be different. This may start from any point in the story and continue to the end;

• key scenes can be replayed in different tenses (past or future).

Drama sessions provide the language teacher with a wealth of information with which to work. We advise teachers to make good use of this. Supplement the drama with language exercises and language practice, looking at issues that have arisen in the drama, cover items you have seen them have difficulty with, and provide them with further vocabulary. We find students learn easily when they can relate grammar to a "live experience", particularly one in which they have been actively involved.

2.4 ADAPTING ACTIVITIES AND TEMPLATES

Since every class is unique and every teacher has her own agenda, you may find it necessary to adapt certain activities or indeed the focus of a template to fit your particular classroom. For those of you who are new to this way of working, we give some guidelines as to how you can do this. In 6.3 we make reference to four templates in order to provide examples as to how this can be done. We suggest that you refer to this section once you are familiar with the template system and the templates themselves.

LANGUAGE ABILITIES

Our Divisions

We are all aware that ways of talking about language ability (knowledge about language) differ between countries, disciplines and theoretical viewpoints. In order to translate the notion of "ability" more readily around the world we make reference in our templates to the broad categories of beginner, intermediate and advanced students. We hope that teachers in classrooms round the world can relate to these and translate them into the way you characterize ability in your own classroom. For the purpose of this book we characterize these levels in the following way:

Beginner
This student may have fairly good comprehension abilities but is limited in his ability to communicate verbally and in writing. There will be lack of control of the **TL** and numerous grammatical errors made. He is able to name objects and perhaps form very simple sentences but little else.

Intermediate

This student may have a good level of oral fluency but still makes errors with tenses and verb agreements. Structure and usage are communicated in a clear but limited manner. He communicates effectively in everyday contexts but needs patience in more abstract concepts. His vocabulary is adequate, although he sometimes needs to paraphrase.

Advanced

This student has good command of the **TL**, can use it in context and only makes occasional errors. His language is natural and appropriate in style; there is some sophistication of language use and usage. He rarely needs to paraphrase.

Techniques for Adapting Activities for Different Language Abilities

With practise, teachers will find it is not difficult to tailor drama activities to students with differing abilities. Often guidance is given in the template as to how to do this. There are also certain techniques that are always useful to remember.
The teacher can:

- take a role to help beginners;
- set the type of language used orally or by introducing information;
- choose different dramatic strategies to match the students' language ability;
- use open dramatic activities to let students of differing abilities set the type of language used in their group (the teacher will either ensure there are mixed abilities in each group or divide students into groups of similar abilities);
- keep a list of recurring vocabulary or important points;
- allow real beginners to use a dictionary.

In 6.3 we give concrete examples of how this can be done with reference to four specific templates.

Activities Which Help You Introduce Language

As we have emphasized already, ideally, in a **drama session**, language should not come to the fore "as a subject" for the student. We have found that when students realise that language is the emphasis they become quiet and inhibited. However, certain drama activities actually allow the teacher to surreptitiously introduce language, For example:

- in a **hotseating** process you can pose a question in a certain form and students will pick up on the tense used and form their own questions in the same tense
- working **in role** you can start a discussion/conversation in a particular tense and the students will follow
- working **out of role** the teacher can talk to the class in the **TL** about what she is doing ... "I will put these props here so that you can...; you can lead a discussion in a **drama circle** using specific language; choose her words specifically in the **guided imagery** exercises, etc.;
- in **puzzle poetry**, you can choose the parts of speech/tense formations included in the cards which will in turn influence the language produced
- when documents/letters, etc., are introduced into the drama, you choose the language students work with

WRITING

Teachers will find that in each template, writing tasks are clearly divided into different abilities. Naturally these are guidelines as you yourself will best know the writing capabilities of your own students. Where various writing tasks are set we have found it useful to begin with writing in role, as this is a natural continuation of the drama and can stimulate excellent work, often where least expected.

LANGUAGE ABILITY MATRIX

We also provide a **language ability matrix** to allow you to see at a glance the different types of competence and ability that come into each drama session. We suggest teachers look at section 7.1 on language abilities which explains the type of "discussing", "listening" or "description" we are talking about as the terms are used specifically in the text.

At the end of each template you will find the same kind of table showing which language abilities come into play for each activity in the drama session in question.

LANGUAGE THEMES TABLE

For those teachers working with set language course books based on themes, this is an "at a glance" guide to which templates can be used/adapted to tie in with general themes commonly used in language teaching.

Life Experiences

Students of Different Ages

Students of different ages offer a range of experiences. In language classes it is often the case that various age groups are represented. You may have to adapt the templates to suit the experiences of a particular age group and in cases of multi-aged groups, consider ways of engaging all students so that they can take away something that is unique to them as individuals.

Remember however that not only children, but adolescents and adults also love to play. Just as adolescents and adults will love to do the *Cinderella* template (which is a fairy story but involves cognitive work), they will also like to make the **soundscape** in the *Weather* template. The difference is in what both you and the students do with the activity. You will for example tailor the language to suit their abilities, giving advanced vocabulary for sounds. They will also be capable of producing some very advanced work if mask work, with words, is introduced into activity 4 in *Weather*. If the teacher decides to use masks these can be simple (made of card) or elaborate (made of plaster bandages and painted); made in the session or in a prior session. Thhis may be carried out in the **TL** or the native language, depending on the students, and so on.

It may also be interesting to solicit and compare different age groups' reaction to parts of the drama — both during and after the session itself. The possibilities are endless.

Students From Different Cultures

Students studying languages other than their own bring with them a variety of interesting cultural backgrounds. Teachers are encouraged to make use of the multicultural atmosphere in their classrooms by incorporating tales, rhymes, anecdotes that are relevant to that particular culture. Cinderella is the perfect example of this as is the adaptation to Old Age — Activity 6.

Different cultures also bring different norms and traditions. As we have already mentioned, some cultures are not used to the physicality that is sometimes involved in drama sessions and some cultures may be more "outgoing " than others. If your students are timid, look for group-improvised dramas which leave open the type of drama students feel comfortable with; choose **stimuli** they can relate to. **Tableaux** are also a good way of getting students moving without the added complication of language. We suggest that once you are familiar with both your class and this way of working, you look at the drama strategies involved in each template and adapt them; if really necessary it is also possible to substitute an activity which you really feel may alienate your students by another with a similar purpose.

Students Who Are Less Mobile

Some participants may be less agile than the others due to age or physical disability. If you know this in advance you can adapt the templates so that sitting on the floor is avoided:

- have chairs round the edge of the room ready to be pulled in for a **drama circle**;
- provide desks round the room for working on in **mantle of the expert** for example;
- let less mobile students become the choral part of the scene whilst others take care of the movement;
- choose your pre-drama activities from the first book in this series, *Drama Games*, which has a lot of activities suited for students with disabilities; or have students sit on the edge of a chair as they carry out movement activities, etc.

Living and Surrounding Environment

The living and surrounding environment of students will also shape their experiences. Teachers can accommodate these students by choosing to work with material that is relevant to the students' everyday lives. Other curriculum areas can also be easily brought in.

For examples of how to personalize the templates to meet the requirements of your individual classroom in this way see sections 2.4 and 6.3.

We now share with you templates formed from lessons learned in our classrooms. Our hope is that they will help make language come to life in your classrooms as they have in ours.

DRAMA TEMPLATES: *SINGLE SESSIONS*

3. 1 SHOPPING

This drama session plays with language by looking at commercials advertising different products for sale.

Stimulus: Student invention.
Class Size: Any.
Props/Materials: Shopping bag.
Preparation: None.
Teacher's Role: Support group work, stimulate ideas.

PRE DRAMA

Language Game: The Shopping Bag

Everyone forms a circle. Pass the shopping bag from person to person and add on to the sentence.

Adapt language used to level of class

Teacher starts:

- Mrs. Carter has been shopping/ is shopping. In her bag there is a packet of frozen peas. Passes bag to next person who repeats and adds on an item.
- Mrs. Carter has been shopping. In her bag there is a packet of frozen peas and a Spice Girls CD. Passes bag to next person who repeats and adds on another item.
- Mrs Carter has been shopping. In her bag there is a packet of frozen peas, a Spice Girls CD and a pair of high heeled shoes ...

Continue round the class. If someone forgets something or gets it wrong, or in the incorrect order, they drop out.

Allocate a set time for the game and then even if there is no "winner", move on to the drama.

Short Lead-in Discussion (Optional)

The teacher leads a short discussion around the following questions:

- Where do you usually shop?
- Who usually does the shopping for your family?
- When you think of "shopping" ... what words would you use to describe ...

Note, any of these questions could be qualified ("Where do you shop for food?" etc.)

DRAMA SESSION

Activity 1: Commercials

Group formation exercise — about 5–8 people per group

Groups are to decide which shop in the shopping mall (shopping centre) they represent. Each shop is one of the places that Mrs. Carter could have bought her goods.

Be prepared for students who may choose a department store to provide all of the articles.

Each shop devises a TV or radio commercial either promoting their produce or their shop. Groups are encouraged to devise a slogan and include dance, song and humour. They can devise their own style or work in the style of a commercial they know for another product. When they have finished working it out they sit down.

The teacher should encourage groups to stand up and try it out rather than sit talking about what to do.

The teacher acts with an imaginary remote control in hand and "turns on" each group at a time, one after the other. When "on", the group stands up and presents their commercial to the rest of the class.

Activity 2: The Competition

Each group chooses another (the shoe group chooses the frozen peas group). The shoe group will then devise another brand of frozen peas or another type of peas to those just presented, say fresh peas grown on a farm. They are then to present the competitor's promotion.

The teacher asks each group to present the commercial **in the style of** EITHER a film/theatre style, a sitcom, a music video, a silent movie, a spy film, etc., OR in the style of an author, a Shakespearean play, Yellow Pages, The Highway Code, The Bible, Grimms Fairy Tales, Disney animal movie, etc.

Activity 3: The Audience

Working in the same groups, each group is asked to choose another product they have not yet tackled and are given a particular audience for whom they have to provide their advertisement, (toothpaste for pirates, mobile phone for elves, pizza for witches, beef stew for vegetarians, etc.).

Adaptation

The class chooses one shop (the supermarket, a men's clothes shop). Working in groups, each group chooses a country and presents the products found in the shop in their country. The products can be presented dramatically (students come forth in role as the product and introduce themselves, they make up a song or choral presentation, they improvise someone going into the shop to buy products, they present an advertisement/commercial, etc.).

POST DRAMA

Writing

Write a creative piece from the viewpoint of the product, i.e. what it is like to be a shoe up for sale; Discuss the pros and cons of a shopping mall/shopping centre; Do you think people will desert shops in favour of shopping on the Internet?

Writing/Visual Work

Devise the advertisement for your product in a woman's magazine or on the Internet.

LANGUAGE ABILITY TABLE

Shopping	Language Ability									Writing Ability						
	a	b	c	d	e	f	g	h	l	1	2	3	4	5	6	7
Language Game: The Shopping Bag		X		X												
Commercials	X	X		X		X										
The Competition	X	X		X		X										
The Audience	X	X		X		X										
Further activities											X			X	X	

Language Ability		
A. Discussing	G. Specialized language	W.4. Formal writing
B. Vocabulary	H. Reading	W.5. Writing for the media
C. Listening	L. Literature link	W.6. Discursive essay
D. Speaking	W.1. Personal writing	W.7. Taking of notes
E. Description	W.2. Creative/imag. writing	
F. Part. Grammar points	W.3. Writing for publishing	

3.2 MEMORIES

This template looks at the power of memories.

Stimulus: Artefact, personal memories.
Class Size: 15+.
Props/Materials: Artefacts, personal belongings (memories).
Art Supplies: Coloured pencils, water colours, wax crayons, clay, paper, etc.
Preparation: Remind students to have memories before this class.
Teacher's Role: Participant, stimulate ideas.

PRE-DRAMA

Any pre-drama activity

DRAMA SESSION

Activity 1: Personal Narratives

Each participant brings to class something that represents a memory. This can be an artefact, picture, story, event, etc. Each participant shares their piece with the group by telling the story of the memory.

This can be explored as a whole class or in smaller groups in the case of large classes.

Activity 2: Story Exchange

Once everyone has shared, participants pair up with someone and share how the memory of their partner reminds them of a similar memory they may have or how it makes them think of something that is related.

Allow participants to change partners at least 3 times.

Activity 3: Reflection

The group gathers as a whole. Each participant is asked to think about all of the memories and to share what thoughts or words come to mind.

Younger students/
Beginners

The teacher may help by asking: How did the memories that were shared make you feel? What did the memories you heard today make you think of?

The teacher keeps a list of these phrases, words, or expressions.

Older students/ Intermediate+	The teacher may ask them to think about the power of memories and what they have learned about themselves and others through these memories.

Each participant or a scribe writes down thoughts on a sheet of paper in the centre of the circle.

Activity 4: Creation of Images

Each participant creates a symbolic image to show what memories (in general) represent for them personally.

Younger students:	Prompt them to: a) think about a definition: what is a memory? and to show this by painting or drawing a picture. OR b) paint or draw a picture of their favourite memory and how it made them feel.
Older participants:	Select from a variety of art mediums from which to work. See the list of materials at the start of the template.

Note: Keep students working in the TL.

Activity 5: Dramatic Expression of Images

Any group formation exercise

Depending on which activity has just been completed, either:

• groups represent their definition of memory dramatically using dialogue; or

• in groups, participants decide on one memory to depict. They are to depict the EMOTION of the memory (e.g., euphoria, sadness, etc.,) using sound and movement but no dialogue.

Note: Words/language may be used in the dramatic presentation but the emphasis is on the presentation of the abstract.

POST-DRAMA

Writing Beginners

Each student dictates a sentence sharing something about the feelings or thoughts expressed in their pictures. The teacher records it below their picture.

Writing Intermediate/Advanced
Using the language generated in the reflection exercise, participants write what it is that a memory means to them. Participants or teacher can choose a genre in which to work. These pieces can be shared and displayed alongside the image work throughout the classroom.

LANGUAGE ABILITY TABLE

	Language Ability									Writing Ability						
Memories	a	a	c	d	e	f	g	h	l	1	2	3	4	5	6	7
Personal Narratives				▓												
Story Exchange			▓	▓												
Reflection	▓	▓														
Creation of Images																
Dramatic Expression of Images	▓	▓					▓									
Writing Activities										▓						

Language Ability		
A. Discussing	G. Specialized language	W.4. Formal writing
B. Vocabulary	H. Reading	W.5. Writing for the media
C. Listening	L. Literature link	W.6. Discursive essay
D. Speaking	W.1. Personal writing	W.7. Taking of notes
E. Description	W.2. Creative/imag. writing	
F. Part. Grammar points	W.3. Writing for publishing	

3.3 OLD AGE

By creating a story about a senior citizen, this drama session looks at what it is like to become old.

Stimulus: Artefact.
Class Size: 10+.
Props/Materials: A piece of string.
Preparation: Prepare vocabulary; go over drama strategies.
Teacher's Role: Help create storyline, stimulate imagination.

PRE-DRAMA LANGUAGE ACTIVITY

Beginners

Students will look at pictures of people and guess how old they are.

Intermediate/Advanced

Students will read a piece of prose or a poem dealing with old age or the problems of being old; or listen to a song about growing old.

DRAMA SESSION

Activity 1: What it is Like to Get Old

Students are asked working either as a whole class, brainstorming, or in pairs who report back:

• when you think of "old people" what words would you use to describe an "old man" or an "old woman"
• how does getting old change your life — physically, emotionally, etc.

Beginners
This exercise can be used to concentrate on the description of people. The teacher could also introduce vocabulary of the body.

Intermediate/+
The teacher leads a short discussion on whether students would consider cosmetic surgery to look younger.

Activity 2: In the Manner of the Word

Students form a circle and take turns to cross the circle in the manner of the word, either as old or young (i.e., tottering across the circle (old); walking very slowly across the circle (old); skipping across the circle (young)).

Further language work: The teacher could introduce work on comparisons, students comparing the "seniors" to themselves.

Activity 3: Creating a Storyline

The teacher passes a piece of string around the classroom which each student in turn makes into something

> *It's not a piece of string, it's a ... snake, it's a ... necklace, it's a ... washing line, crown ... etc ...*

Students show the object dramatically, moving the string like a snake, putting it round their neck like a necklace etc.

The teacher or scribe writes these things down on the board. Either the teacher or the students and teacher together make up a description of a scene or beginning of a story involving a senior citizen and all of the objects.

Activity 4: Overheard Conversations

The class decide upon a few characters who will know about the senior person — their nurse, their relative, the butler, the maid, the milkman. Volunteers take these roles and they choose someone to be their pair. In turn each pair improvises a conversation about the senior person or something strange or exciting that has happened involving them. The rest of the class have their eyes closed whilst the pair speak. They imagine they are overhearing the conversation. The teacher may take a role to help.

Students are reminded we are trying to find out what it is like to be old and to develop the description/storyline. Bring in the objects in the description/story. Each pair is to be encouraged to build upon what the others have said or to link their conversation to the storyline.

The teacher or scribe writes down what is found out as the story unfolds.

Activity 5: Interviews

Divide the class in two, forming two concentric circles. Half of the class forms a circle facing inwards, half of the class faces outwards, so that each person faces a pair. The outside circle are told they are the reporters, the inside circle the old person. Reporters are given a set time to ask the old character questions related to what they have learned from the **overheard conversations**.

Note: Teacher can give the example and set the tense. This can be made very simple or quite complicated, depending on the type of question and the tenses used.

The information learned is shared with the rest of the class.

Note: This may take the story off in different directions; if possible they should be drawn into one story, if not consensus must be reached as to which information remains in the story.

Activity 6: Tableaux, Captions

Group formation exercise — we need a group big enough to portray the initial picture/storyline created with the piece of string.

This group create a **tableau** of the description/beginning of the story.

The rest of the class form smaller groups. Each group is to think of the viewpoint of the different characters that have been involved in the drama — the old person, the characters in the **overheard conversations**, other people in the scene. Each group creates a **caption** (title/headline) for the **tableau**, representing the different viewpoints of the different characters.

Adaptation: How Do Different Cultures Treat "Seniors"

The teacher asks students to contribute information from their own culture by leading a discussion which could begin with the questions:

• do you live with your grandparents? or do they live with you?
• how often do you see your grandparents?

The class divides in two. Each half prepare an improvised scene including a senior person from a particular culture which tells the class something about the essence of being a senior in that culture. They share it with the other group.

Intermediate/Advanced

The questions could revolve around: — How do women grow old in your culture? How do they dress/act? Compare this information with life for the older woman in the culture of the **target language** or that of another continent. Groups of students can present the information dramatically via **improvisation**.

POST-DRAMA

Writing

Write a page in the old person's memoirs relating to one of the activities in the drama. If a storyline was begun, develop the story. How do you feel about growing old? "My Lonely Hearts Ad" (max 50 words; "My Obituary " (max 50 words).

Beginners

Write the description of the **tableau**.

Intermediate +

Go and interview someone who is a senior citizen and find out what they see as the pros and cons of being their age.

Drama

Signing the Space: Create an area in the house or a place the character often visits that tells us something about them — somewhere where there are things to be read: books (titles), perhaps lists (anything from a shopping list to a list of things to do), letters etc.

Time Line: Class is divided into groups. Each group decides upon an age during the life of the person. Each group presents a **tableau** or improvises a scene of an important moment in the old person's life. Alternatively the time line could look at the last 5 to 10 years of the person's life.

LANGUAGE ABILITY TABLE

Old Age	Language Ability									Writing Ability						
	a	b	c	d	e	f	g	h	l	1	2	3	4	5	6	7
What it is Like to Get Old					■											
In the Manner of the Word		■				■										
Creating a Storyline		■														
Overheard Conversations			■		■											
Interviews	■		■													
Tableaux	■		■													
Captions						■				■		■	■			
Further Activities										■	■	■	■	■		

Language Ability		
A. Discussing	G. Specialized language	W.4. Formal writing
B. Vocabulary	H. Reading	W.5. Writing for the media
C. Listening	L. Literature link	W.6. Discursive essay
D. Speaking	W.1. Personal writing	W.7. Taking of notes
E. Description	W.2. Creative/imag. writing	
F. Part. Grammar points	W.3. Writing for publishing	

3.4 BUILDING ONE MINUTE STORIES

This is a fun way of getting students to build short stories.

Stimulus: Language work.
Class Size: Any.
Props/Materials: Any.
Preparation: None.
Teacher's Role: Stimulate imagination; keep momentum.

PRE-DRAMA

Any pre drama activity

DRAMA SESSION

Activity 1: Brainstorming

The whole class brainstorms what types of stories there are and what elements are important in story. They also consider:

• structures for playing with story
• strategies for working in story
• ways of reflecting/learning from story/story journey (writing, re-telling tale, questioning/discussing)

Activity 2: Given Circumstances — Who? Where? When?

Group formation exercise into groups of three. One person in each group supplies:

who? — a sense of characters involved
where? — a sense of the location where story unfolds
when? — a sense of time of day and/or historical epoch

Activity 3: What Happens Next?

Once these given circumstances have been established, group members build a one-minute story:

• one word at a time, or
• one sentence at a time or
• one phrase/paragraph at a time

Activity 4: Changing Places

In the same groups another story is built. Each group member provides a different element of the given circumstances, i.e.,

who? (Person No.1) where? (Person No.2) when? (Person No.3)
who? (Person No.2) where? (Person No.3) when? (Person No.1)
who? (Person No.3) where? (Person No.1) when? (Person No.2)

Adaptation

Depending on the language level of the students, this can be further varied by either: giving each group a specific genre for their story (e.g., mystery, romance, thriller, horror) or letting them choose their own genre.

POST-DRAMA

Further activities   Stories can be written down/tape recorded/ videotaped, etc.

Students can be asked to suggest ways of reflecting on/learning about story/yourself through story.

LANGUAGE ABILITY TABLE

Building One Minute Stories	Language Ability									Writing Ability						
	a	b	c	d	e	f	g	h	l	1	2	3	4	5	6	7
Brainstorming	▓															
Given Circumstances — who? where? when?	▓															
What Happens Next?	▓	▓		▓												
Changing places	▓	▓		▓	▓											
Further activities	▓									▓						

Language Ability		
A. Discussing	G. Specialized language	W.4. Formal writing
B. Vocabulary	H. Reading	W.5. Writing for the media
C. Listening	L. Literature link	W.6. Discursive essay
D. Speaking	W.1. Personal writing	W.7. Taking of notes
E. Description	W.2. Creative/imag. writing	
F. Part. Grammar points	W.3. Writing for publishing	

3.5 NURSERY RHYMES

This drama session explores and extends a familiar nursery rhyme or fable.

Stimulus: Classical nursery rhyme or short fable.
Class Size: 10+.
Props/Materials: Collection of nursery rhymes.
Preparation: Select suitable rhymes or tales to be used — here we use "Little Miss Muffet".
Teacher's Role: Raise questions, guide the process.

PRE-DRAMA

Any pre-drama activity

DRAMA SESSION

Activity 1: Introduction and Discussion

a)   The teacher asks students to think about a time where they were afraid of something. The teacher may begin the discussion by sharing first. As the class shares, the teacher or **scribe** makes notes of the emotions felt in the various situations.

b)   The teacher recites the rhyme "Little Miss Muffet" and asks the class to think about why she might be so afraid.

Activity 2: Storytelling and Mime

a)   The teacher recites the rhyme as the class acts it out, using movement only. Students will all be working at the same time in their own space. As the teacher recites the rhyme, she uses thought **tracking**. She calls **freeze** at various points to ask individual students questions. The teacher taps the students on the shoulder to let them know they are being asked. For example:

Little Miss Muffet
Sat on a Tuffet, (freeze)
   how big is that Tuffet you're sitting on?
   how does that Tuffet feel?
   what does your Tuffet look like?
Eating her curds and whey; (freeze)
   how often do you eat curds and whey?
   who made the curds and whey for you today?
   where can you buy curds and whey?

Along came a spider (freeze)
are you afraid of spiders?
have you ever seen such a spider before and
*   where?*
what does this spider look like?
And sat down beside her (freeze)
what do you think that spider wants from you?
if that spider could talk to you what do you think
*   it would say?*
And frightened Miss Muffet away.

Activity 3: Capture the Moment:

Use any group formation exercise to form pairs

Students work in pairs, one plays the role of Miss Muffet and the other of the spider. In a **tableau** each pair shows what happens after Miss Muffet is frightened away.

Note: Younger students will need reminding not to talk, but to show.

Activity 4: "I Wonder"

The teacher raises a question regarding the events in the rhyme or story. (e.g., I wonder where the spider came from? I wonder what the spider likes to eat?).

The students raise their own questions about the rhyme using "I wonder". The teacher keeps a record of the questions, and a list of possible answers.

The students can draw the answers (e.g., the spider crawled out of the water jug, the spider likes to eat bananas, ice-cream, and pizza.)

Younger students can dictate the words for the teacher to write below their drawings. Older students can use the vocabulary recorded.

Adaptation

Students can be asked if there is a similar rhyme or fable in their own culture. If so they can share it with the class.

See also our Cinderella Across Cultures Unit for examples of a drama unit built around a story which spans many cultures.

POST-DRAMA

Drama

Divide the class in half. One half is little Miss Muffet, and the other half is the spider. Imagine that it is the next day and the spider comes back for another visit. What might the two of them talk about?

Writing/Visual Work

As a class, the students create a class booklet entitled: "What to do to protect yourself from a spider." Each student illustrates one page for the book and offers a piece of advice on how to protect yourself. The teacher assembles all of the ideas into a class booklet to be shared with the whole class.

LANGUAGE ABILITY TABLE

Nursery Rhymes	Language Ability									Writing Ability						
	a	b	c	d	e	f	g	h	l	1	2	3	4	5	6	7
Introduction and Discussion	▓				▓											
Storytelling and Mime		▓		▓												
Capture the Moment	▓															
"I Wonder"	▓					▓										
Further Suggested Activities						▓								▓		

Language Ability		
A. Discussing	G. Specialized language	W.4. Formal writing
B. Vocabulary	H. Reading	W.5. Writing for the media
C. Listening	L. Literature link	W.6. Discursive essay
D. Speaking	W.1. Personal writing	W.7. Taking of notes
E. Description	W.2. Creative/imag. writing	
F. Part. Grammar points	W.3. Writing for publishing	

3.6 THE LION'S DEN

This drama session looks at moral and practical issues as the animals decide whether to stay in the wild or move to a zoo.

This template can form one lesson or be divided over two sessions, depending on how long the teacher wishes to spend on the language work at the beginning.

Stimulus: Student invention.

Class Size: 12+; suitable for larger classes.

Props/Materials: Poem about lions (see bibliography), music, animal songs (see bibliography); music apparatus.

Preparation: Prepare literature and music, review dramatic strategies.

Teacher's Role: Stimulate discussion and analysis, keep order!

PRE-DRAMA

Poem, song or text about animals (see bibliography for ideas)

Poem: we suggest *"The Monkeys and the Crocodile"* (Laura E. Richards) in Ferris, H (Ed) (1957)

Music: any song about animals that will engage with the language and age level of the students. It should be as catchy as possible.

DRAMA SESSION

Activity 1: Introduction — The Animal World

The following should be a series of short, sharp activities

a) What animal are you/ what animal would you be?

In circle, teacher asks the students:

Beginners: You are an animal, what animal are you, what animal are you like?

Intermediate+ If you were an animal, what animal would you be?

Adapting language to the level of the students, the teacher can begin by saying something like I am/I would be a bear because I am big and fearless and I have big hands and feet. Someone continues — I am a wild horse because I am a free spirit running with the wind ... I am a duck because I like to swim...

b) Animal noises or animal groups:

Younger students: The teacher asks what kind of noise the animal makes and gives the vocabulary for it: a lion roars, a pig squeaks, etc.

Older students: The class learn the vocabulary for groups of animals: a flock of sheep, etc.

c) Animal Habitat: Each person is asked to describe the habitat they live in: I am a penguin and I live in the cold. I like to slide down the ice into the water and look for fish to eat, etc.

d) The Laws of Nature: The class is divided into animal groups such as pets, farmyard animals, wild animals in accordance with their own choices.

Each group is asked to work out the relationships between their type of animal and another someone else has invented (the dog chases the cat; the cat is afraid of the dog; the cat catches the mouse; the mouse runs away from the cat). Every animal must be included.

If time allows the relationships could be presented dramatically. Pieces are shown to the rest of the class.

*The teacher should help by suggesting different dramatic methods: chorus, narration over mime, **improvisation** etc.*

Activity 2: Working in Role: The Lion's Den

a) The teacher informs the class they are going to work **in role**. If someone chose to be a lion bring them forward and get them, **in role**, to repeat what they have said about themselves or found out about themselves. Get the class to describe what this lion looks like — is it a male with a long mane or a female with honey coloured skin, etc.

A poem could be introduced here. We suggest Lizzy's Lion, by Dennis Lee in Patten, B (ed.) (1991) and/or The Lion and the Echo, by Brian Patten in Harrison, M & Stuart-Clark, C (1990). If no one chose to be a lion move to 2.

b) The teacher asks for two volunteers who stand aside (with younger classes teacher might like to take this role).

The teacher then informs the rest of the class they are a community (pride) of lions. One volunteer is the zookeeper and the other his *helper* (or teacher plays role of zookeeper with no helper).

c) The teacher tells the lions that they live in a fertile valley beside the forest but that mysteriously some of their cubs keep disappearing every night. The bodies never appear. However much the parents try to guard their cubs some always disappear. This is getting to be a very desperate situation.

The zoo keeper and his helper are visiting soon to ask them to go to the zoo. This is to be carefully considered in a meeting as a safe option.

The class decide who are the lions, who are the lionesses and who are the cubs (or use a group formation exercise to divide class into three) — and who is their chief. Each group of lions can have various roles in the pack — the head of the hunting lions, the head of the pack's babysitter, the cub's chief lioness of education, head of the environmental lion's society, etc.

Each group is given a few minutes to discuss and decide (1) whether they want to go to the zoo and (2) why/why not. Each group must come to a decision — yes, or no. When they are ready they sit down and wait for the zoo keeper and helper to arrive, gather as for a meeting, not sitting at desks.

The zookeeper and helper are to prepare their argument to offer the pack safety in the zoo — permanently.

The teacher's role is to keep this short as the real argument is to take place in the meeting in activity 3.

Play music in background as they do this (e.g., atmospheric music from Disney's Lion King).

Activity 3: The Meeting

Teacher sets up meeting. The chief lion acts as "throneperson" for the meeting. He will make the final decision. The zookeeper and his helper present their offer. Then spokesperson in each group presents their case.

The teacher takes the role either of a lion or the zookeeper and keeps the argument moving.

Activity 4: Voices in the Head

The chief lion is given space to think.

He sits on the floor and the class sits either to the left or the right of him. Left means — we go to the zoo; right means — we stay at home. The person nearest to the lion holds his hand. In turns someone from left or right speaks as his alter ego voicing either why they should go/why they shouldn't or yes you must go/no you mustn't. Each time a side speaks the person pulls on his hand and draws him their way so that the lion is made to sway back and forth, yes/no; yes/no.

The teacher should monitor that this does not get too rough.

Should everyone sit on one side the teacher takes the other and acts as devil's advocate.

Activity 5: The Decision

The chief lion stands up and ROARS his decision.

Happy music (e.g., "Hakuna Matata" chorus from *The Lion King*) played.

POST DRAMA

Writing

Pamphlet for or against animals in zoos, article on "Life in the Wild", Petition to the chief lion against his decision, book on lions — different groups covering different topics, write a poem in role as a lion/lioness/cub, "Born Free": should animals be kept in captivity?

Drawing

Draw a picture that encapsulates 1) the meeting 2) how you feel about the meeting and the chief lion's decision.

Drama

TV report on the lion's meeting and decision.

LANGUAGE ABILITY TABLE

The Lion's Den	Language Ability									Writing Ability						
	a	b	c	d	e	f	g	h	l	1	2	3	4	5	6	7
Poem/Song								■								
Introduction — The Animal World		■		■	■	■										
Working in Role: The Lion's Den	■			■												
The Meeting	■			■												
Voices in the Head	■															
The Decision				■												
Further Activities												■	■	■	■	

Language Ability		
A. Discussing	G. Specialised Language	W.4. Formal writing
B. Vocabulary	H. Reading	W.5. Writing for the media
C. Listening	L. Literature link	W.6. Discursive essay
D. Speaking	W.1. Personal writing	W.7. Taking of notes
E. Description	W.2. Creative/imag. writing	
F. Part. Grammar points	W.3. Writing for publishing	

MARIANNE JEWELL MEMORIAL LIBRARY
BAKER COLLEGE OF MUSKEGON
MUSKEGON, MICHIGAN 49442

3.7 ABSTRACT ART

This template uses art to make meaning and build a story.

Stimulus: Evocative picture or abstract art.

Class Size: 10+.

Props/Materials: This strategy can be explored in two ways: in small groups (you need one piece of art for each group, same or different or as a whole class: you need one piece of art preparation, review dramatic strategies, particularly guided imagery).

Teacher's Role: Stimulate imagination, guide the process.

PRE-DRAMA

Any pre-drama activity

DRAMA SESSION

Activity 1: Building Imagery and Mood Through Guided Imagery

a) Participants study the picture or multiple copies of the picture.

Provide ample time for all to examine the art work carefully.

b) **Guided imagery** (See appendix)
Participants work independently. Teacher asks students to close their eyes, step into the picture and think about what they feel, see, etc.

c) Personal Images
Each participant SILENTLY creates a pictorial map, design or web of all of the images that were created from the guided imagery exercise and not necessarily a replica of the art work.

Participants should be given several minutes to draw.

The teacher then asks students to call out images (such as light, smoke, damp, wind, heat, shadow) as they continue to work on their illustrations. The teacher makes a list of all of the images on the blackboard. These can be used later.

Any group formation exercise (groups of 3–5)

Activity 2: Character Development

Participants in each group decide who they want to be in the picture. They adopt the role of that character. Working in their groups, **in role**, each character shares three things about themselves. Each member of the group asks the character at least one more question.

Note: It is important that the teacher allows enough time for characters to develop.

Activity 3: Developing Plot

a) In the same groups, the participants (**out of role**) discuss possible reasons why or what has brought the group together in this situation.

b) Each group prepares a **tableau** showing the rest of the class the relationship between all of the characters and why they are here at this time. The groups are advised that in this **tableau/still image** some kind of message is being communicated.

Note: The teacher should tell the students the aim is to provide tension (mystery, secrecy, spies, gossip, obstacle, etc.).

c) In turn, each group presents their **tableau** to the rest of the class. The other class members can be invited to use **thought tracking** to find out more about the situation and the message.

Note: The teacher should remind participants to focus their questions on the task of finding out more about the story that surrounds the message being communicated.

Continue this process until all groups have presented.

Activity 4: Overheard Conversations

a) **Out of role**, the groups decide on one character to come to life to communicate to the others.

b) Each group, in turn, sets up their **tableau** again. The rest of the class can now hear one side of the communication. Other members of the **tableau** remain in freeze positions whilst the communicator comes to life. The communicator shares a bit of knowledge or information that the audience may not already know from the **tableau** work.

Activity 5: Caption Making

The audience suggest **captions** (headline, chapter heading, song title etc) for each presentation.

The teacher or a **scribe** records these. Repeat with each group.

Activity 6: Different Accounts

The class choose one situation to develop.

Group formation exercise: If numbers suit, members of the group whose situation was chosen divide and each becomes head of a group.

a) Groups devise and show what happened next, based on their knowledge of the characters but developing their account from the viewpoint of ONE CHARACTER.

The teacher should help with possible ways of dramatizing and emphasize that there may not always be a resolution to the situation.

Intermediate/Advanced students only continue with:

Activity 7: Giving Witness

a) Each character gives a highly subjective monologue relating events from their point of view.

b) **Caption Making**
Captions are made for each presentation. These are recorded as before.

c) The audience chooses "the real story" which may be based on one of the **captions** presented here and on **overheard conversations** or a combination of both.

Time should be made here, or in a later session, for discussion / reflection on the differences between all of the interpretations of the art, the stories and the different captions and how they have contributed to the development of the stories.

POST-DRAMA

Writing

- Differing responses: Students look at the relationships between stories and their tellers either with relation to literature or different types of media or different publications for different audiences.
- Each student writes two or more different responses to the same situation by different tellers for different audiences.
- Write the resolution to the story (should there not have been one) or to one of the stories not further developed.
- Write a poem relating to the image work and the words generated at the beginning of the drama. This can relate to any parts of the session that followed, or it may suggest a whole new message not communicated in the session.

LANGUAGE ABILITY TABLE

Abstract Art	Language Ability									Writing Ability						
	a	b	c	d	e	f	g	h	l	1	2	3	4	5	6	7
Building Imagery and Mood Through **Guided Imagery**:			▓													
Character Development		▓		▓												
Developing Plot	▓															
Overheard Conversations			▓	▓												
Caption Making						▓										
Different Accounts	▓			▓												
Giving Witness	▓					▓										
Further activities										▓						

Language Ability		
A. Discussing	G. Specialized language	W.4. Formal writing
B. Vocabulary	H. Reading	W.5. Writing for the media
C. Listening	L. Literature link	W.6. Discursive essay
D. Speaking	W.1. Personal writing	W.7. Taking of notes
E. Description	W.2. Creative/imag. writing	
F. Part. Grammar points	W.3. Writing for publishing	

3.8 DRAMATIC APPROACHES TO TELLING STORY

This drama session looks at how drama can convey story in many different ways.

Stimulus: Brainstorming.
Class Size: 8+.
Props/Materials: None.
Preparation: Prepare explanation of story.
Teacher's Role: Stimulate imagination.

PRE-DRAMA

Any pre-drama activity

DRAMA SESSION

Activity 1: Brainstorming

The class is asked to identify the different elements that make up story. The teacher writes up all the answers on the board in the form of a large **web**, guiding students where necessary and helping with vocabulary.

Students are asked to brainstorm the **elements of story** (e.g., structure has beginning, middle, end; characters need to be interesting, need to create suspension of disbelief in audience, etc.) as completely as they can. The teacher can decide to help or fill in any of the gaps.

The teacher explains that:

• every story is a journey
• if it is a good story it will pull the audience along the journey
• things must happen to make story work: facial expressions, actions and movement, voice, synchronicity or disynchronicity.

Activity 2: Telling the tale

Group formation exercise — 5 to 6 students

Each group is asked to think about story ideas. Teacher gives each group a specific manner of presentation (e.g., Chorus work with sound, images, tempos; or with poetry rather than prose).

Chorus and leader (narrator)
• narrator provides focal point

Chorus, leader (narrator) and actor/character **in role**
• group(s) decide where the focus will be

Chorus, leader (narrator) & 2 actors/characters in **role**

The groups are told to choose one well known story, folk tale or fable and to use these as a model, presenting their own stories in the structure of the known one. If necessary one person can play more than one character. Groups are reminded to co-operate and to keep it simple, to ask themselves: Is it interesting? Why do we want to tell this story?

The groups practise and then present their story to the rest of the class.

Activity 3: Discussion

Class discusses the general structures of story (Chorus to modern theatre).

In the classroom it is easy to lose the focus of the story and focus instead on pairs, small groups, or the class itself. The teacher emphasises that it is important to remember in concentrating on structure not to lose part of story: character, setting/ time/ place, plot, beginning/ middle/ end, action.

LANGUAGE ABILITY TABLE

	Language Ability									Writing Ability						
Dramatic Approaches To Telling Story	a	b	c	d	e	f	g	h	l	1	2	3	4	5	6	7
Brainstorming	█	█														
Telling the Tale	█		█													
Discussion	█													█		

Language Ability		
A. Discussing	G. Specialized language	W.4. Formal writing
B. Vocabulary	H. Reading	W.5. Writing for the media
C. Listening	L. Literature link	W.6. Discursive essay
D. Speaking	W.1. Personal writing	W.7. Taking of notes
E. Description	W.2. Creative/imag. writing	
F. Part. Grammar points	W.3. Writing for publishing	

3.9 COMMUNICATION IS THE KEY

Note: This is a good follow-up template to Dramatic Approaches to Telling Story

This template focuses on how we communicate information. It can be useful in helping students to understand how and why conflicts may arise.

Stimulus:	Student discussion.
Class Size:	10+.
Props/Materials:	None.
Preparation:	Suggested statements for "Do you mean what you say?"
Teacher's Role:	Review strategies (forum theatre), lead discussions, guide the process.

PRE-DRAMA

Any pre-drama activity

DRAMA SESSION

Activity 1: Brainstorming

The teacher begins by discussing various ways we communicate (i.e., voice, body language, expressions, emotions). The teacher expands on these by asking the class to list various ways in which we use them when we are trying to communicate a message.

The teacher or **scribe** may generate a list as ideas are shared.

Activity 2: Do You Mean What You Say?

a) Students work in partners, A & B.

b) The teacher provides a series of statements or questions (i.e. I really like your hat, Did you enjoy your dinner? That film was terrible. Are you planning to go to the party?) Partner A repeats the statement selecting various emotions and expressions from the list in Activity 1. Partner B replies to the statement.

c) Repeat this so that both partners get a chance to express the same statement/question and respond in a different way.

d) Repeat this by practising several statements/questions.

Activity 3: Discussion

Based on their experience with Activity 2, the class share how tone, voice, gestures, facial and body expressions and emotions have an effect on what they are trying to communicate.

Activity 4: Creation of Scenarios

Depending on the size of the class this can be done as a whole class or in small groups.

a) Participants list a variety of settings where people gather (i.e. restaurant, grocery store, doctor's office, etc.). Using the list of settings from a) include appropriate characters and create short scenarios involving some kind of problem (i.e., couple enters a restaurant 5 minutes late for their reservation to discover that their table has been given to another couple.)

b) Participants record these scenarios on cards so that they can be circulated among various groups.

Activity 5: Forum Theatre

a) Select one of the scenarios created and ask a group of students to improvise a scene around the situation. Allow the group to run through the entire scenario once with out interruption.

Note: Set a time limit for the improvisation

Using **forum theatre** techniques the audience intervene in order to *change the way the character communicates*. The scene must continue on to the end.

This exercise can be repeated several times with the same or different scenarios

b) The class discusses how communication affected the outcome of the scenario(s).

POST-DRAMA

Writing

Write the dialogue (or key sentences/main speech) from one of the scenarios **in the manner of the word** (i.e., apologetically, angrily, etc.). The teacher should allocate the adverbs.

Time should be taken to go over the type of language used in each situation and to compare different students' renderings of the same scenario with different adjectives.

Drama

Activity 1: Conflicts

Teacher asks the class to think about a time they may have disagreed with a friend, employer, family member, teacher etc. Each student independently records a list of words and images expressing the thoughts and emotions they might have felt during that particular situation.

Group formation exercise: groups of 4

Activity 2: Peaceful Resolutions

In groups students share their stories and present their work. Each group, selects one conflict to explore further (there may be common threads in the stories presented).

Each group works together to use humour as a way of communicating a message for a peaceful resolution. According to the level of group, the teacher may discuss various ways humour can be used (i.e., story, riddle, joke, slogan, satire, metaphor).

Activity 3: Reflection

The students refer to their work in Activity 1 and transform that language to design a bumper sticker, poster, or pamphlet, to promote peaceful resolutions.

Related Writing

Write a letter to the employer, friend, or relative one year after the conflict. Write a script based on resolving a conflict peacefully. Prepare this for presentation to a young audience (perhaps using puppets).

LANGUAGE ABILITY TABLE

Communication Is The Key	Language Ability									Writing Ability						
	a	b	c	d	e	f	g	h	l	1	2	3	4	5	6	7
Brainstorming	X															
Do You Mean What You Say?	X		X			X										
Discussion	X															X
Creation of Scenarios	X					X										X
Forum Theatre		X	X													
Further Activities	X	X				X				X	X	X		X		

Language Ability		
A. Discussing	G. Specialized language	W.4. Formal writing
B. Vocabulary	H. Reading	W.5. Writing for the media
C. Listening	L. Literature link	W.6. Discursive essay
D. Speaking	W.1. Personal writing	W.7. Taking of notes
E. Description	W.2. Creative/imag. writing	
F. Part. Grammar points	W.3. Writing for publishing	

3.10 TRAPPED BEHIND ENEMY LINES

This drama session sets students in an improvised spy mystery in order to play with language through passwords and guessing games.

This template can be done in small groups (3–5) or in a large group, depending on the wishes of the teacher and the size of the class. It begins with the simulation technique of assigning characters to participants via cards. Our template however differs from simulation in that participants use the card as a starting point from which to develop their *own* character.

Stimulus:	Personal cards.
Class Size:	12+ — suitable for larger groups.
Materials:	Cards with one of the following on each:
	— SPY
	(*name* + Secret password and Contact's response)
	— CONTACT
	(*name* + Spy's Secret password and response)
	(various cards)
	— ENEMY AGENT, ASSASSIN
	— PROSTITUTE, BY-STANDER, etc.

If the template is done as one large group there can be 1 or more Spies and their Contact.

Preparation:	Make cards.
Teacher's Role:	Create atmosphere, maintain tension.

Note: It is very important that the teacher creates a mood of suspense and real 'terror', perhaps by discussing inappropriate behaviours and the consequences of being caught. It may help if the group share some of their own real life experiences, or what scares them. The template will not work if students play for laughs or do not take this seriously.

PRE-DRAMA

The teacher guides a group discussion around the group's own scary experiences, or what it is that frightens them.

Any pre-drama activity

DRAMA SESSION

Activity 1: Describe Your Ideal Date

The teacher asks the students to describe their ideal date, in accordance with their language level — (s)he is/would be ... and (s)he will/would take me ... (i.e., he is tall, dark, with nice eyes and a sense of humour and he would take me somewhere where we could both talk and have fun).

Activity 2: Given Circumstances

The teacher informs the participants that they have a very special kind of "date" today. In fact, they are going to change time, place and character in order to meet that "date".

The teacher informs the participants that there is/are a spy (spies) trapped in a foreign country and if they are caught they will be killed! They have a very important secret in their possession which they *must* get out of the country. The teacher informs them that they are going to be a part of this mission. The teacher explains that participants are to take on and develop the character on the cards which they will be given. They have to meet their contact at a public gathering (e.g., Intermission at an Opera, half-time at a major sporting event).

This can be set by the teacher or can be suggested by the group

BUT they have never met this person. They do not even know if their contact is a man or a woman. All they have is their secret password and their contact's response.

These need to be on the Spy and Contacts cards

e.g.: Spy: Do you enjoy cabbage and beetroot pizza?
Contact: Yes, it is delicious with Vodka don't you think?

Teacher distributes cards and gives participants time to read and digest the contents.

Adaptation

For Intermediate/Advanced or older students only:

The Government agent and/or the assassin have gained possession of ½ of the coded message or some part of it (e.g., either: Do you like to rub your body with cabbage? or: Only in a bath of slivovitch...).

Activity 3: Making Contact

The teacher creates the atmosphere of the event the class has chosen as the contact place and the Spy drama starts rolling. The aim is for the spy to meet the contact. A wink or sign can be given once they have met each other. They have to find some way of escaping.

*The teacher may intervene **in role** if the drama needs moving on. The teacher should encourage the class to **suspend disbelief***

Adaptation for Intermediate/Advanced Students
Additional complication: ***Before the drama*** each partner has to write a State (or Personal) secret and try to pass it to a partner who they can only identify with a predetermined password. This password would need to be written on a card using the card format above.

Post-Drama

Writing
Discussion: All participants at the gathering write a 50–100 word synopsis of what happened. These ideas are then shared as a group;

Tell me about the secret you have to get out of the country and why it is so important. Recount what happened after you left the gathering.

In role as the spy describe your hiding place. Write the opening page of a spy thriller. What do you think of double agents? Write a page in the biography/memoirs of the spy/contact/enemy agent.

Drama
The class is divided in two groups, A and B. Group A tell/read group B their version of what happened in the improvisation and Group B has to try to recreate the events of the evening.

LANGUAGE ABILITY TABLE

Trapped Behind Enemy Lines	Language Ability									Writing Ability						
	a	b	c	d	e	f	g	h	l	1	2	3	4	5	6	7
Describe Your Ideal Date		▓		▓	▓											
Given Circumstances			▓			▓	▓									
Making Contact				▓												
State Secrets							▓									▓
Further Activities	▓						▓					▓	▓	▓		▓

Language Ability		
A. Discussing	G. Specialized language	W.4. Formal writing
B. Vocabulary	H. Reading	W.5. Writing for the media
C. Listening	L. Literature link	W.6. Discursive essay
D. Speaking	W.1. Personal writing	W.7. Taking of notes
E. Description	W.2. Creative/imag. writing	
F. Part. Grammar points	W.3. Writing for publishing	

3.1 1 MY GRANDFATHER

This is a **storydrama** which takes a *story* as its base. The story could be something that has happened to one of the participants or part of a film or play they have seen. In this type of story drama what is important is that the tale has a sense of person, place, time and purpose. However it should leave *out* details so that a range of possibilities come into play.

Stimulus:	Incomplete story.
Class Size:	5+; suitable for large classes.
Materials:	Story (see appendix), music (Yiddish, Russian or other suitable music) musical instruments, assorted articles that could be a part of the story.
Preparation:	Know tale well.

The teacher may come with a story already chosen or prepared in a previous session. She can have asked participants to provide stories which may be used. A well written and well constructed story will speak across gender and across culture. The teacher should select the story to ensure it has many different dramatic possibilities.

Teacher's Role:	To engage interest in the tale at the beginning, encourage participants to think about the uses of story, and to help participants look at how to enter and develop a story.

We suggest that teachers who have not done this type of drama before should use our template and the given materials.

PRE-DRAMA

Any pre-drama activity

DRAMA SESSION

Teacher's Introduction

The teacher explains that in this drama they will be looking at ways of telling or retelling a tale. They will be looking at the uses of story, the notion of taking story out of context and the shape of the story.

Activity 1: Telling the Tale

Teacher tells or reads the tale entitled "My Grandfather" (see appendix).

Activity 2: Analyzing the Tale: Brainstorming

The Teacher leads the brainstorming under the following headings:

a) Analyzing the Tale

The teacher uses dramatic questions to explore the tale. By asking students who? where? when? what? ... students can explore the how? and the why? of the tale.

This can lead students to explore the tale under the following headings:

b) Retelling the Tale

c) Finding Dramatic Moments to Enter the Drama

Participants should come to the conclusion that the tale tells the bones of a story, giving us a taste of events, but leaves out many missing details.

Adaptation for Intermediate/Advanced Groups

Students work in small groups to brainstorm the tale they have been told. Participants could be asked to write this down, or to write notes.

Activity 3: Personal Reflection

Participants retell the story and the teacher makes them realize that they have not been given the names of the characters, any notion of what else is happening, what happened to those left behind, what the route of travel was or what they took with them, etc. What they do know is that this is a history of a family, the success of moving, the history of a people in a particular part of the Ukraine.

In the **drama circle** participants are asked to think about what they personally got out of the story. The teacher explains the importance of finding a story that works for you personally. The teacher explains that the class is now going to look at ways in which they can make the tale their own.

Group formation exercise. Small groups of 5-8 people are formed.

Activity 4: Dramatic Moments

The teacher tells the groups they can investigate any dramatic moment or any part of the story that they wish. They can enter the tale at any point in time, set it in the past, present or future. They can introduce new characters, change the focus, expand, tell the story from different points of view, relate it to their own lives. What they must do is make the tale and the expression of the particular part they have chosen, *their own*. Groups are reminded to keep it simple.

Activity 5: Retelling the Story Dramatically

Groups are asked to retell the story. Each group is given a way in which to tell it, for example:

- **Narration.**
  Narrator tells the story, embellishing the dramatic moments. Members of the group act out what happens. Soft Yiddish music is played in background.
- **Tableaux.**
  The group uses **tableaux** to recreate dramatic moments. Other characters take it in turns to call other characters, one at a time out of the tableaux. These characters, **in role** are asked about the story — both with relation to the **improvisation** they have participated in and to other parts of the story.
- **Mime** (with or without music/sound effects).
- **Guided Imagery**.
  The group retells the story adding in rich descriptions whilst others listen with their eyes closed.

Adaptation

Advanced groups can be asked to choose how they want to present the dramatic moment chosen.

The teacher's role is to move from group to group and help/ guide when necessary with both ideas and ways of dramatizing them. She should also enforce the TL rule.

Examples of what some of our students did with the tale. Points of entry:

- A Town meeting is called to decide whether to leave or stay.
- The mother tells her story of being married to an alcoholic during these troubled times.
- The Market Place — problems of immigrants.
- Prejudice — stressing the family's fear and country's hatred.

- Historical family tree — tale of family through three generations. People tell the tale but fit it to their own time period.
- Leaving scene — what should they take with them.

LANGUAGE ABILITY TABLE

My Grandfather	Language Ability									Writing Ability						
	a	b	c	d	e	f	g	h	l	1	2	3	4	5	6	7
Teacher's Introduction			■													
Telling the Tale			■													
Analyzing the Tale: Brainstorming	■															
Personal Reflection	■			■												
Retelling the Story Dramatically	■			■												
Dramatic Moments	■			■												

Language Ability		
A. Discussing	G. Specialized language	W.4. Formal writing
B. Vocabulary	H. Reading	W.5. Writing for the media
C. Listening	L. Literature link	W.6. Discursive essay
D. Speaking	W.1. Personal writing	W.7. Taking of notes
E. Description	W.2. Creative/imag. writing	
F. Part. Grammar points	W.3. Writing for publishing	

3.12 EMIGRATION

This drama session looks at what it means to emigrate to another country through improvised scenes around an invented story.

Stimulus:	Artefacts.
Class Size:	10+ — suitable for large classes.
Props/Materials:	A trunk/suitcase full of articles wrapped in brown paper and string The objects should be old and suggest a character (e.g., an old pair of glasses, a sepia photograph, a worn out teddy bear, a strange necklace, etc.) hats, a brown paper package not in the case.
Preparation:	Prepare parcels, revise different ways to develop a theme dramatically.
Teacher's Role:	Encourage students to keep the story going.

PRE-DRAMA

Any pre-drama activity

DRAMA SESSION

Activity 1: The Trunk

The teacher introduces the trunk and the theme. For example:

> *"Many people move to lands far away from where they were born and make them their home. Where is it that people from *name of country students live in* go to? Why do they go there? ...*
>
> *"... This trunk was washed up on a far shore and belonged to an interesting person. Inside are artefacts all belonging to this person, indicative of who they were and why they decided to emigrate."*

Participants take it in turn to go up to the trunk and take out an artefact and unwrap the parcel.

Writing

In pairs, participants write either as the character or the artefacts themselves, explaining their part in the character's life . Each pair takes it in turns to read aloud what they have written and to show their artefacts to their colleagues.

Adaptation
Lower-level students can write just adjectives.

Building a Character
Participants in circle then guess to whom the suitcase might belong. Ideas are written up on the board and as a group, than all participants choose one of the suggestions.

The teacher's role is to bring everyone to a decision without taking too long and thus losing the power of the drama story being developed.

Activity 2: Class in Role

The teacher produces another brown paper package. **In role** as the owner of the trunk, she explains that this package was kept with her all through the journey because it was too important to be left in the trunk. The parcel is passed around everyone in the circle. As this is passed round, each student, in turn, steps into the circle **in role** as the traveller and says what is in this package which they kept with them throughout the journey.

Activity 3: Interviewing

Group formation exercise — class divided into two

The class forms two circles, one facing inwards, one outwards. One circle is formed of journalists, the other of the character just invented. The journalists **interview** the emigrant, changing places when the teacher indicates so that each journalist gets to speak to three different people in role . Then the emigrants and journalists change roles and the same happens. The journalist is to find out as much as possible about why the character is emigrating.

Class forms one circle again. Journalists are invited to share the best stories they have heard. The class chooses two to pursue (or one if the class is small).

Adaptation
For lower-level students this activity can be replaced by **hotseating** the character. Continue with the story that emerges from the **hotseating**.

What some of our students have done with this:
• It is 1950. A mother goes to Auschwitz where her son was killed, taking with her his prayer book which is all she has left of him. She intends to pray for him beside his grave and make Germany her home.

- A British girl leaves home because she does not get along with her stepfather. She goes to New York with nothing but her doll to seek her fortune.
- A spy is travelling to Russia to look for his missing daughter. He carries the only photograph he has of his daughter with him.
- An author is fleeing from the country where his book is banned. He carries his book with him.
- A refugee is leaving her homeland forcibly due to war. She carries a box with some earth of her homeland with her.

Activity 4: Dramatic Moments

Group formation exercise — two groups, (if numbers allow, each subdivided into three)

Each group produces a **tableau** which develops into an improvisation of three dramatic moments.

a)   Home: either showing reason why leaving; or parting scene
b)   Dreams of success
c)   Reality: any problems/conflicts have to deal with

The participants can choose to present story or abstraction (e.g., the turmoil of leaving, or the way in which a mother left her family to go on her search for her missing son). The teacher tells the groups they need to include the article in the package which is important to them.

The teacher's role is to encourage different forms of dramatization, to encourage use of light, music, song, mime or dance as well as words. N.B. If the class is really large two groups can collaboratively deal with each three points, one via story the other via abstraction (e.g., fear/uncertainty, euphoria, disappointment/relief).

POST-DRAMA

Writing
Write a letter to a friend explaining why he or she should or should never come to your new country. Write the entry in your diary a week after arriving in your new country explaining why it was/was not a good idea to move.

LANGUAGE ABILITY TABLE

Emigration	Language Ability									Writing Ability						
	a	b	c	d	e	f	g	h	l	1	2	3	4	5	6	7
The Trunk	▓		▓			▓										
Class in Role		▓	▓	▓												
Interviewing	▓			▓												
Dramatic Moments	▓															
Further Writing									▓							

Language Ability		
A. Discussing	G. Specialized language	W.4. Formal writing
B. Vocabulary	H. Reading	W.5. Writing for the media
C. Listening	L. Literature link	W.6. Discursive essay
D. Speaking	W.1. Personal writing	W.7. Taking of notes
E. Description	W.2. Creative/imag. writing	
F. Part. Grammar points	W.3. Writing for publishing	

3.13 QUEST: A JOURNEY DRAMA

In this **storydrama** students continue a story given by the teacher in which they go on a collective quest, **in role**.

Our quest is inspired by J.R.R. Tolkien's *Lord of the Rings* as a source for our quest, but any story dealing with a journey could be adapted. The students may or may not have read the book chosen. You as teacher should decide whether you prefer for them to have done so or not.

Stimulus: Story.

Class Size: 15+ — suitable for large classes.

Props/Materials: You may want to use a passage of text from your chosen book (i.e., for our quest you may want to use the Ancient Prophecy, see *Lord of the Rings* Frontispiece).

Teachers may need to modify this for lower-level students. Teachers who are familiar with drama may like to improvise their own text and slightly change the story to suit their needs.

A bracelet (any will do but an "interesting" one is best), tools to create atmosphere (e.g., a wizard's staff (optional), visual — candles/fairy or Christmas lights, audio-sounds-tambourine/chimes/bells/xylophone/maracas/background music).

Preparation: Review different strategies that can be used to develop the narrative.

Teacher's Role: Provide vivid stimuli, break drama tasks into different, sequential tasks, decide which steps will be taken to explore the question.

*Set up story so that students can develop the narrative but give the students the power to decide how the action develops. Intervene **in** or **out of role** if students need help with language or drama development. Encourage group work. If you have not done this type of drama before we suggest you follow the template below.*

PRE-DRAMA

Any pre-drama activity

Drama Session

Activity 1: Teacher's Introduction

The teacher explains that the group is going to tell a story together. This story has no single solution. The group together will come to a consensus as to what is acceptable and what is not. The beginning is given by the teacher, but it must be played through collectively to its end. Participants will need to defend why they are playing who they are playing (context and content) but will NOT predict what will happen.

Activity 2: Setting the Scene

The teacher's role is to set up the story. The time, setting, characters and main points that are to be dealt with are given and the solution to the problem is left open. At this point it is important to create atmosphere and suspense to **build belief**.

For example, candles, fairy lights or dimmed lights could be used, depending on the space/age of the participants. Music or sounds could be introduced.

Teacher In Role

In role, teacher tells initial story (modify language to suit class):

> *I, have bad news.*
> *The Dark Lord has returned.*
> *He has already gathered many of his dark forces to him.*
> *Many others are waking and will soon join him.*

Teacher in role (**TIR**) as The Grey Wizard explains that a bracelet is an essential object for this particular hero/journey quest. The Grey Wizard searches for the bracelet and brings it out to show the class.

TIR as The Grey Wizard continues:

- The Great Bracelet must be destroyed. If it falls into the hands of the Dark Lord he will rule us all.
- Whoever wears the bracelet becomes invisible. But the bracelet is very dangerous and very powerful. In the end it will completely overcome any mortal who has it in their possession.

Activity 3: Starting the Quest/Adoption of Characters — Improvisation

The Grey Wizard asks for volunteers to take the role of travellers to begin the Quest. These travellers will work as a group:

TIR (modify language to suit class)

* I need a small group to help carry the bracelet, to accompany the bracelet carrier. It must be a small group to avoid detection. The group must travel without being noticed. If this group fails we all are doomed.
* So I ask you all — elves, dwarves, fairies, and all the races of humankind gathered here today which of you will accompany the Bracelet Carrier on this Quest to destroy the bracelet? I need volunteers. Please step forward and tell me who you are.

Volunteers come forward.

The number of travellers will depend on the size of your language class. We suggest between 5-7 travellers in a class of 25-35.

The teacher, **out of role**, explains that each traveller has a special power. The teacher gives volunteers time to talk in a group and decide what their special power is.

The rest of the class are asked to start to think what could happen to the travellers on their dangerous quest.

After a short, fixed time limit, the teacher asks the travellers to state their special power to the class. **In role** travellers step forward and state their name, their heritage and their special power to the rest of the class.

(optional) One or more member(s) of the group could be given an artefact which has special powers which must not reach the hands of the other side. The rest of the class may or may not be informed about this.

Once all travellers have stepped forward, the teacher shouts — **freeze Thought tracking.** Participants are asked what travellers are thinking as they begin their quest.

Story Building
TIR asks travellers

* what they are taking with them on their quest and why?
* how they intend to destroy the bracelet?

Activity 4: Group Work

TIR explains there will be perils to be overcome.
The teacher is now **out of role**

Group Formation Exercise
The rest of the class is divided into groups. Each group thinks of an obstacle that the group of travellers needs to overcome on their quest.

Groups and travellers could be asked to write this down.

Activity 5: Group Dramas

Each group creates their obstacle for the travellers to overcome. The teacher goes round from group to group to see if everyone fully understands and helps if necessary. The teacher then decides the order in which each obstacle will be presented to the group of travellers.

The teacher explains that if the travellers need help, the rest of the class (the audience) can help travellers out when their obstacle isn't in play.

*Note: Usually the travellers do ask for help, or the teacher, seeing that they are "stuck" calls **freeze** and asks for suggestions from the audience. Occasionally the teacher may decide to enter the scene **in role** as a character to aid the travellers.*

The travellers enter a series of improvised situations prepared by the groups, introducing their particular obstacle.

The teacher can decide to use one or all of the following techniques to develop the narrative in accordance with a) their ability in the **TL** b) drama experience c) age/experience of participants d) class time.

1. **tableaux**
2. **auxiliary ego/voices in the head**
3. **role reversal**
4. **discussion in groups**
5. **sound/lights**

Below we give examples of obstacles from experience. The teacher's role is to limit time/extend time spent on each point and each group, to encourage development of points of interest and to keep the narrative flowing. Note there is no right answer. The teacher's role is to sway the drama in a workable direction. The teacher may decide to use some of the techniques in the glossary or to introduce language work.

Remember there should be time for each group to present their obstacle so that the whole class is involved. Make sure that each group is aware of how to use the space. It may help for the action to take place within a circle.

Since the possibilities are endless, teachers will need to work with what it is the students give them, direct the audience (i.e., play out only the essential action, make the text/action accessible to all language levels/age groups).

Note: Do not allow students to give too much information. This must come from the development of the action and not be pre-described, or there is no room for creativity and belief in the character/role. Barriers should be formed with the idea of being clever/taxing and not to kill the drama by presenting an obstacle that cannot be passed. The aim is not vengeance but complication.

Activity 6: Thought Tracking

The teacher shouts **freeze** and asks travellers or audience questions using a certain tense — e.g., What are you thinking? What can the travellers do? What do you think will happen next?

The teacher can use this to introduce new and necessary vocabulary. Note: Be careful not to interrupt the drama too much. It should flow.

The teacher asks the audience to describe the emotions that the travellers must be feeling (e.g., excitement, worry, frustration, joy).

The teacher or **scribe** notes down summary of events (e.g., Travellers arrive at the forest). They are cold and hungry...

Examples of what our students did with GROUP DRAMAS:

1. Forest of Poisoned Apples
   The group is poisoned by apples and no longer able to use their powers.

2. Audience Intervention
   The audience are asked to intervene and help. For example: a witch enters who makes everyone sick. The travellers' powers are thus resumed.

3. Divide and Conquer
   Group introduces village and welcomes travellers to rest there. Villagers begin to lie to the travellers about each other to force them against each other.

(N.B. The villagers should plan the end or they could have a strong conflict on their hands). Travellers resolve lies through discussion in groups.

4. Unresolved Conflict
   Another conflict is added that they cannot leave the village with the bracelet.

Example ending: Group is found to have a leader. Travellers resolve conflict by turning the villagers against each other; distracting them to sneak away.

5. Physical Obstacle
    Rock Bridge — Only six out of the seven travellers can pass through; or a dragon and a poisonous river have to be defeated and crossed

POST-DRAMA

Drama
Go back to a moment of tension. Set up the scene with **Voices in the Head**.

Writing (Beginners)
Write down the emotions the travellers felt on their journey. Write a letter home telling what happened.

Writing (Intermediate)
Write an entry in your diary the day before you go on your quest. Write a letter to be opened by your spouse only if you do not return from your quest.

Writing (Advanced)
Choose one of the obstacles and explain a way in which it could be resolved differently. Tell the story of how your own group of travellers met an obstacle during the quest. Write the editorial in the newspaper about the quest. The teacher uses a quote from the book which relates to what the students have done to stimulate an essay. Students who have read the book introduce their obstacle into the book and then see how the characters would resolve it. Students put one of their characters into the book or one of the book's characters into their drama.

Language Ability Table

The Quest	Language Ability									Writing Ability						
	a	b	c	d	e	f	g	h	l	1	2	3	4	5	6	7
Teacher's Introduction			■													
Setting the Scene			■													
Starting the Quest	■		■													
Group Work	■															■
Group Dramas	■		■		■											
Thought Tracking	■		■													
Further Activities	■	■								■				■		

Language Ability		
A. Discussing	G. Specialized language	W.4. Formal writing
B. Vocabulary	H. Reading	W.5. Writing for the media
C. Listening	L. Literature link	W.6. Discursive essay
D. Speaking	W.1. Personal writing	W.7. Taking of notes
E. Description	W.2. Creative/imag. writing	
F. Part. Grammar points	W.3. Writing for publishing	

DRAMA TEMPLATES: *UNITS*

4. I WEATHER

This unit uses the theme of weather in the news to move from sound to the dramatization of stories based on specific weather conditions.

There are two sessions, A and B. A is particularly suitable for young students but is also a valuable warm up exercise for adults who will spend more time on Session B.

SESSION A

Stimulus:	Music.
Class Size:	10+.
Props/Materials:	Music combining or imitating the sounds of the elements (rain, wind, thunder, etc.) or nature (birds, dolphins, etc.).

Teachers can tailor the music to the group.
(See appendix for ideas.)

	Music apparatus: a selection of articles and headlines from various daily newspapers that are weather related, miscellaneous materials, household items that can be used for creating sound makers that express the sounds of weather and nature for the **soundscape** (popcorn kernels, rice, beads, elastics, macaroni, tin cans, containers, cardboard or paper tubes, simple masks and fabric remnants for movement and language exercise. Optional.).
Preparation:	Select appropriate atmospheric music.

Teacher's Role: Facilitate discussions, stimulate ideas, generate vocabulary.

PRE-DRAMA

Any pre-drama activity

DRAMA SESSION

Activity 1: Active Listening

a) Participants find a spot on the floor where they can sit or lie down comfortably. The teacher asks them to close their eyes whilst they listen to a piece of music

b) The teacher asks participants to think about the various sounds, thoughts, or emotions that enter into their minds and to identify these while they are listening.

c) The teacher keeps a list of ideas and may categorize the responses under various headings depending on what the group is sharing. For example: elements, sounds, emotions, nature, other.

Adaptation

Beginners: Review the list of words and create phrases by combining words from different categories. (i.e. The loud rain frightened me).

Intermediate/Advanced: Create several opening lines to a possible short story. (i.e. The heavy rain startled me. As I jumped out of bed to shut the window, a flash of lightning struck the big oak tree that stood outside my bedroom...)

Activity 2: Weather in the News

a) The teacher shares a few T.V. or news headlines that inform of weather conditions in the area or around the world. The group chooses one to explore further.

b) The teacher, in role as newsreader, gives the report for that headline to the class.

Adaptation
Beginners: After reading, the teacher can add any significant vocabulary to the list generated in the first exercise.

Activity 3: Vocabulary Building Through Soundscape

Participants work together as a whole group (or two large groups depending on the size of the class) to create a soundscape of the event described in the article or story. The elements and sounds can be taken from the list that has been generated thus far.

a) Participants make the **soundmakers**
Some ideas for interesting sounds:
> balloons filled with water or popcorn kernels;
> toilet paper tubes filled with rice;
> camera film containers filled with beads;
> plastic containers filled with popcorn kernels;
> tin cans filled with elastics.

The teacher may want to take advantage of this opportunity to explore vocabulary for sound. (crash, ring, rattle, bang, swish etc.) Such as, the wind rattles the windows, my feet swish as I walk in the rain.

b) Participants experiment with putting the sounds together to create a soundscape. They start by practising the sounds individually, then together.

The teacher should also encourage them to explore by increasing and decreasing the intensity.

Activity 4: Movement and Language

Group formation exercise (class divided into two)

One group continues with the soundscape to either a crescendo or decrescendo. The other half, working as a group, portray the music with their bodies, through movement and through the use of language. For example, participants adopt the role of wind, rain, etc... The use of simple masks and fabric remnants may add to the mood of the movement piece. Words (such as those in the list) can be added to the movement, whispered or shouted in accordance with the mood.

The teacher may allow the use of a dictionary here to help with vocabulary work, but emphasis should be given to movement rather than passive dictionary work.

Repeat this exercise so that each group can experience both.

Note: This session is particularly good for creating a wealth of vocabulary. Make sure participants create or are given a list of the vocabulary learned.

POST-DRAMA

Writing Beginners
Write a postcard home describing the weather. Write down several adjectives that remind you of each season (e.g., spring — fresh, brisk; summer — hot, hazy; autumn — nippy, colourful; winter — snug, damp. Link these adjectives to nouns and verbs to write a piece about each season. Write a **cinquain** using the list above.

Writing Intermediate
Write a weather advisory to warn the public of expected weather conditions.

Writing Advanced
Write an evocative piece (prose or poetry) about the season you like best. This piece could also be written from the point of view of the elements, the wind, the snow etc; Write an essay entitled "The Powers of Nature." Write a short story based on the story openers from Activity 1.

Literature link
Teacher introduces a piece of poetry dealing with a particular season. See our appendix for ideas.

SESSION B

Stimulus:	Storytelling.
Class Size:	10+.
Props/Materials:	A variety of articles that can be used in different weather conditions (umbrella, sunglasses, mittens, raincoat, boots). Soundmakers from previous session.
Preparation:	As session A.
Teacher's Role:	As session A.

PRE-DRAMA

Group formation exercise (groups of about 5)

Pre-drama activity: Improvisational warm up: The teacher gives each group a prop and asks them to improvise a situation where the prop is used. The rest of the class have to give a title to the piece.

DRAMA SESSION

Activity 1: Storytelling

Participants sit in a circle. They are asked to think about an incident where the weather has affected their life. This can be something recent or remembered from long ago. The teacher may give an example to start off.

Activity 2: Recording

The teacher or a **scribe** keeps a chart with the following headings:

Weather	Affects/Effect	Who	Where	When
wind	messed hair	me	hair salon	wedding day
tornado	baby in the car	mother and child	driving	dusk
torrential rain	plans	couple	beach resort	honeymoon
lightning	couldn't ride water slide	kids	water park	family vacation
scorching sun	hike up mountain	us	in the mountains	school camp

The teacher should encourage participants to generate as many scenarios as possible as this will make possibilities for follow-up activities more interesting. These can be serious or humorous.

Activity 3: Dramatizing the Action

Group formation exercise (groups of about 4–5).

If numbers permit half of the groups are assigned a) "silent movie" and half are assigned b) "comic strip stories". If numbers do not permit teachers can choose to do one or both of the exercises.

Both exercises work with, add to and expand the scenarios already presented. Soundmakers can be incorporated in both a) and b).

Silent Movie
In activity 2, Who, What, When, Where have already been named. Groups need to decide on what other characters could be part of this story. The groups working on a) work as a team and prepare scenes but they are to be presented in the silent movie format.

Note: The teacher should explain that this is not mime, it is a STORY in mime, encouraging the participants to deal with plot. No speech is allowed but sounds are.

The teacher plays camera (wo)man and focuses her camera on each group in turn. When in focus, each group presents their scene. They stop action as the camera scans over to the next group and the next group begins.

Comic Strip Stories

The teacher should make it clear that the challenge is being able to tell a story in a few frames, not necessarily to make it comical.

Participants should devise four scenes around one scenario on the class chart. These scenes should deal with key points in the story — a beginning, an end and two middle frames.

Note: The same group may provide all four scenes or four groups can each present a scene, depending on the size of the class. The scenes should include movement and speech.

The comic strip should then be presented to the rest of the class.

Adaptation

Younger children may find it easier to divide a piece of paper into four quadrants and write or draw the main points they want their story to tell.

POST DRAMA

Writing

Write the script for the silent movie (dialogue). With reference to one of the scenarios, write a letter to your local newspaper complaining about the troubles caused by the recent weather and the failure of the local council to deal with it. Write about one particular extreme of weather in your country and how it affects daily life. For example when it is very cold and freezes, it is difficult to get to work, trains are delayed, road gritters have to grit the roads, animals are in danger etc. (optional) Then compare the way your country deals with the problem to other countries (many Dutch crave cold weather so they can skate the eleven cities. When the canals freeze thickly enough eleven cities are joined and a national skating race takes place round the eleven cities).

Write a pamphlet for the general public on how to deal with extreme weather conditions such as flooding, tornados, avalanches or forest fires. These pamphlets should be issued by competent authorities such as the fire brigade or the forestry commission.

Grammar

The teacher prepares a **cloze** dealing with the subject of the sessions (the teacher can delete key words that have been dealt with in the sessions from a weather report and get students to fill them in).

Drama

Weather forecast (oral presentation, specialist vocabulary). Participants prepare a televised weather report for the weather channel regarding the weather in one of the scenarios on the chart. This can involve making the charts for presentation.

This may require the students to do some research watching various T.V. stations, in the TL and in their own language(s), to examine how meteorologists present the weather forecast. If differences appear these could be highlighted.

Teachers can broaden this activity by creating language activities such as listening comprehension — letting students listen to a weather bulletin and jotting down the main points, etc.

Specialist vocabulary needs to be learned: humidity, low pressure, etc.

LANGUAGE ABILITY TABLE

Weather	Language Ability									Writing Ability						
	a	b	c	d	e	f	g	h	l	1	2	3	4	5	6	7
Active Listening		▓	▓	▓												
Weather in the News	▓															
Vocabulary Building		▓		▓												
Movement and Language																
Writing Exercises		▓											▓	▓		
Literature Link								▓								
Improvisational Warm Up						▓										
Storytelling					▓											
Recording																
Dramatizing the Action	▓															▓
Further Suggested Activities					▓											
Language Ability	▓				▓					▓			▓	▓	▓	

Language Ability		
A. Discussing	G. Specialized language	W.4. Formal writing
B. Vocabulary	H. Reading	W.5. Writing for the media
C. Listening	L. Literature link	W.6. Discursive essay
D. Speaking	W.1. Personal writing	W.7. Taking of notes
E. Description	W.2. Creative/imag. writing	
F. Part. Grammar points	W.3. Writing for publishing	

4.2 MISSING PERSONS

This drama unit uses questioning and a mystery story to engage students in collaborative solving of a crime.

Format: Storybuilding session with optional end-ings.

Stimulus: Evocative picture for storybuilding.

Class Size: 15+.

Props/Materials: Any evocative picture that includes a person. Try to select one that offers mystery; see our bibliography for ideas.

Preparation: Review use of teacher **in role**.

Teacher's Role: Build belief in drama, stimulate question and response, guide and facilitate discussions.

PRE-DRAMA

Any pre-drama activity

DRAMA SESSION

Activity 1: Story Building

a) **Brainstorming**

The teacher shows the picture to the class and begins asking questions about it. In this case the teacher raises questions to help establish the history of the person in the picture.

➤ Do you know this person?

➤ Where have you seen them before?

➤ What can you tell us about them?

The questions can become more specific such as:

➤ Where were they last seen?

➤ What were they doing?

➤ Where were they going?

➤ Who were they with?

b) **Teacher in Role — Mantle of Expert**

Teacher in role as Chief Investigator Rodney of the local police department, introduces himself and announces that he has just received a missing persons report, identifying the person in the picture as missing. He asks them as investigators in his team to assist by using their skills to help find the missing person.

Investigators are now encouraged to ask questions regarding the case. TIR gives deliberately vague responses in order to lead the students onto their own inquiries.

c) **Discussion/Negotiation:**
   TIR asks his team what jobs need to be done in order to help find the person. TIR makes a list of all of the ideas.

Note: The TIR as chief investigator should take the lead in helping the class negotiate which is the logical action to take, whilst still allowing the drama to be theirs.

The drama that follows depends on the list that the participants make.

The teacher can steer them in the direction of one of the suggestions, or follow one idea this session (day one) and another in a subsequent drama session (day two).

We have found that two suggestions reoccur. These are presented here as an ongoing unit, divided between two sessions.

OPTION A Collecting Evidence (day one)
OPTION B Finding Witnesses (day two)

The two possibilities work as follows:

OPTION A: Collecting Evidence

Activity 1: Collecting Evidence in Role

Group formation exercise (groups of three)

Class, in role as investigators, are told that today is the day after the person went missing.

a) Each group discusses where they would go to find evidence and decides upon one piece of evidence that they have collected.

b) Participants draw and describe the piece of evidence found. Each group selects someone to draw, someone to record the description of the evidence, and someone to present the details to the rest of the class.

c) Each group presents these reports to the rest of the class. These are later posted around the classroom so that everyone can see all of the evidence that was discovered the day after the person went missing.

Activity 2: Piecing the Evidence Together

a) Each group prepares a brief scenario using two pieces of evidence showing what might have happened. Students may select any two pieces that have been found as a result of the whole class' investigation. Students may continue to work in groups of three or the teacher may create larger groups. We suggest no more than five.

b)   Each group presents their scenario to the rest of the class.

Activity 3: Discussion

Out of role, the class chooses **one** of the scenarios presented that they wish to continue exploring in option B. The teacher should act as arbitrator.

POST-DRAMA

Writing

Based on the scenario selected by the whole class, and in role as investigators.

Beginners/Intermediate: write in their log, describing the evidence found and what they think may have happened to the person.

Advanced: write their formal report.

OPTION B: FINDING WITNESSES

PRE-DRAMA

Any pre-drama activity

Note: If carried out on the same day, omit these activities.

DRAMA SESSION

Activity 1: Who can help?

a)   Recap story:
      The class verbally recaps the scenario that they decided to explore from the previous session.
      Key points from the scenario can be listed for students to refer to if necessary.

b)   Based on this scenario, the teacher leads the group in generating a list of characters that may be able to shed some light on the mystery of the missing person.

c)   The class together decide on 3–5 KEY characters from this list that would be able to provide valuable information.

d) A group of students are needed to play the role of the characters selected. They can be volunteers or chosen by the teacher. The rest of the class return to their roles as investigators.

e) The key characters introduce themselves to the rest of the group and prepare to answer questions that the investigators ask. The teacher at this point can play the role of chief investigator in order to facilitate questions and answers and ensure that the story that develops makes sense.

After sufficient answers have been generated:

Group formation activity (groups of 4–5)

Activity 2: Crime Scene

Each group of students recreates a possible crime scene based on the information gathered from the interview. This may be shown through a tableau or a prepared scene.

Post-Drama

Writing

Beginners: Participants create the poster placed in the city offering a reward for the missing person. Write the parents' TV appeal for the missing person.

Intermediate/Advanced: Using one of the scenarios in Activity 2 and in role as reporters, students write a news report describing the case of the missing person. This news report can be for a serious or a sensationalist newspaper or a TV news broadcast, but the writer must stipulate which. Write the investigator's log. In role as the missing person, write down your thoughts (**more specific instructions can be given in accordance with the scenarios invented**).

LANGUAGE ABILITY TABLE

	Language Ability									Writing Ability						
Missing Persons	a	b	c	d	e	f	g	h	l	1	2	3	4	5	6	7
Behind the Story	▓					▓										
Collecting Evidence in Role	▓		▓													▓
Piecing the Evidence Together	▓		▓													
Discussion	▓					▓										
Writing	▓												▓			
Who Can Help?	▓		▓													
The Crime Scene	▓		▓													
Further Writing										▓				▓		

Language Ability		
A. Discussing	G. Specialized language	W.4. Formal writing
B. Vocabulary	H. Reading	W.5. Writing for the media
C. Listening	L. Literature link	W.6. Discursive essay
D. Speaking	W.1. Personal writing	W.7. Taking of notes
E. Description	W.2. Creative/imag. writing	
F. Part. Grammar points	W.3. Writing for publishing	

4.3 THERE ARE TWO SIDES TO EVERY STORY

This drama unit takes a well known fairy story or cultural tale and examines a perspective different to the norm, specifically that of the antagonist. Here we have used Little Red Riding Hood.

Format: Two sessions, A and B.

Stimulus: Any familiar fairy tale or fable that is familiar to the whole class.

Class Size: Maximum of 25.

Props/Materials: None.

Preparation: Select tale that everyone knows, perhaps by discussing fairy tales in pre-session work.

Note: This preparation may not always be easy if the class is multicultural. Check for differences in the same tale across cultures (see our Cinderella matrix in the appendices).

Teacher's Role: Participate in role; guide the process.

SESSION A

PRE-DRAMA

Any pre-drama activity

DRAMA SESSION

Activity 1: Introduction

Teacher retells the original tale or leads a short discussion to highlight the key points to the story (4 or 5 maximum).

Note: For purposes of this drama, if you are using a version where the wolf is killed at the end, you will need to change the ending to show that the wolf is not dead.

Group formation exercise — groups of no more than 5

Activity 2: Collaborative Storytelling

Each group dramatizes one of the key points in the story so that as a class the whole story is told.

Activity 3: Teacher in Role

a)   Teacher in Role invites members of the community to a meeting and tells of her friendly relationship with the wolf.

Teacher in Role as friend of the Wolf begins in this vein:

"Thank you all for agreeing to meet with me at such short notice. My name is (name) and I live in the city (use the name of a city close by). I am here to let you all know that (name of wolf) is safe and is staying at my home. I know you are all probably wondering where he ran off to after that terrible ordeal at granny's house last week. I'm here to tell you that I have been a good friend of (name of wolf) for some time. You see, he comes to the city every Tuesday evening and, as we speak, (name of wolf) is at my house too embarrassed to come back to his own home. He won't eat, he just mopes around the house all day and it breaks my heart. I've come here today to find out what really happened and to find out how you all feel about this situation."

b) In order to establish a history for the character of the wolf, the Teacher in Role invites the community members to introduce themselves and to share a piece of information regarding (name of wolf). My name is (name) and I (tell about occupation). I (share something that you know about (name of wolf).

c) The Teacher in Role invites the community members to ask her questions. She is vague in her responses but insists that (name of wolf) appears to be in a state of depression, and expresses her concern

Allow only a few moments for this questioning to occur.

Activity 4: Discussion

a) The teacher, out of role, facilitates a discussion by asking the class to share all that they know so far about the wolf based on what they have heard so far.

The teacher or **scribe** keeps a list.

b) The teacher invites the participants to share any thoughts or unanswered questions with the group, using the structure "I wonder why, who, what, where, when..."

The teacher or scribe adds to list.

c) The teacher informs the students that it may be possible to discover answers to several or perhaps all of these questions.

SESSION B

Props/Materials: Object to represent the wolf for hotseating process.

PRE-DRAMA

Any pre-drama activity

DRAMA SESSION

Activity 1: A Day in the Life

Group formation exercise — groups of 4 or 5

Each group prepares a series of three scenes (morning, noon, and evening) presenting a day in the life of the wolf. The day in question is the 24 hours preceding the event in the story, in this case the visit to the granny's house.

The scenes are shared with the rest of the class.

Activity 2: Class Discussion

The class choose a scenario to explore further.

The teacher should refer the class to the "I wonder" questions raised in Activity 4.

Activity 3: Meeting

Either:

a) Interviewing the protagonist:
The wolf is invited to a community gathering so that members of the community can ask the wolf questions. Teacher or student may play the role of the wolf.

OR

b) The teacher dims the lights, to commence a modification of the **hotseat**. The community members are asked to take turns to speak aloud and share their thoughts/feelings regarding the wolf. In this case the wolf could be represented by an object placed in the drama circle.

Group Formation Exercise: Create groups of equal number and try to create an even number of groups.

Activity 4: Montage

a) Two groups work together - group A and group B.

Group A will support the original version of the tale and group B the wolf's version. Group A recalls and presents the original version as presented in the first activity. Group B observes and prepares "dialogue only" for the scenes they are watching. This dialogue will be based on the wolf's perspective of the story.

b) Group A presents their original story, with their own dialogue. Group A repeats their story in mime while group B fills in the dialogue.

Repeat this until all pairs of groups have presented.

Activity 5: News Photograph

In the same groups, prepare a photograph that could be used in the local paper to best show what REALLY happened that day at old granny's house.

POST-DRAMA

Writing

Write the news story that goes with the photograph in Activity 5. Brainstorm suitable titles for a new version of this original tale.

Write a statement on behalf of all wolves in various tales from all over the world claiming that they have been misunderstood for too long.

Write a letter as a wolf to another wolf from another tale or story telling about your life and your story.

Create a brand new version of any original tale. Write a biography for one of the antagonists from various familiar tales.

Drama

In pairs, students interview and report about the story as it really happened. A is the interviewer and B is a community member. Switch roles and partners so that everyone gets a chance at playing both roles.

Use the interviews from above to write articles for a local newspaper, defending either side of the story.

LANGUAGE ABILITY TABLE

There Are Two Sides to Every Story	Language Ability									Writing Ability						
	a	b	c	d	e	f	g	h	l	1	2	3	4	5	6	7
Introduction	X		X													
Collaborative Storytelling	X			X	X											
Teacher in Role	X															
Discussion	X					X										X
A Day in The Life	X			X												
Class discussion	X															
Meeting	X	X		X	X											
Montage	X			X												
News Photograph	X															
Further Activities	X		X				X		X				X	X		

Language Ability		
A. Discussing	G. Specialized language	W.4. Formal writing
B. Vocabulary	H. Reading	W.5. Writing for the media
C. Listening	L. Literature link	W.6. Discursive essay
D. Speaking	W.1. Personal writing	W.7. Taking of notes
E. Description	W.2. Creative/imag. writing	
F. Part. Grammar points	W.3. Writing for publishing	

4.4 DRAMATIC EXPLORATION OF STORY: CINDERELLA

This drama unit looks at different cultural versions of the same story. Here we use Cinderella.

Format: Different sessions which are flexible.

Since different levels and age groups will work at different speeds teachers should decide how many sessions to use for their particular class.

Stimulus: A story which differs across cultures: we use Cinderella as there are many culturally different versions of the story.

Class Size: 12+.

Props/Materials: Select several versions of the same story, each from a different culture.

If Cinderella is used, copy and refer to the matrix (in appendix).

Preparation: Know stories and cultures explored in the session.

Teacher's Role: Guide discussions, provide (access to) cultural information.

PRE-DRAMA

Pre-Drama work: familiarizing participants with the given stories (as below)

Younger Students

The teacher reads a different version of the story each day with the class and keeps a chart of the differences as the stories are shared (using matrix as guide).

Similarities and differences can be noted as the process of sharing the different versions continues each day.

Pre Drama Movement Activity
After each story has been shared, students dramatize the story in 5 or 6 scenes. Students may dramatize through mime, with dialogue, storytelling, tableaux, etc.

Older Students

Pre Drama Movement Activity
Each group reads a different cultural version of the story and finds a way to present a short (five minute) dramatized synopsis of the

story to present to their colleagues. After all the stories have been covered participants, in groups, discuss the similarities and differences within the tales as shown by the presentations.

DRAMA SESSIONS

SESSION A

Note: If this takes place on a different day to the pre-drama work a pre drama movement activity should precede the session. If not, the session should continue directly on from the above so as not to break the flow of the story.

Activity 1: Decision Taking

In a drama circle students are asked to think about the main characters in the stories they have read and decide if they wish to explore that of the heroine or the hero. The majority vote rules.

Note: Two options for Activity 1 now follow although the teacher may decide to cover both options in different drama sessions.

Activity 2 Option 1: Exploring Character: The Heroine — Cinderella

Cinderella Meeting
The class form groups of Cinderellas from various tales to discuss and compare the tasks they have been given to do before they meet their Prince.

Brainstorming
Cinderellas find a way of making their jobs easier for them. This may involve designing a tool to help them with their work or developing a strategy or plan of action.

Testing and Presentation of the Plan
Cinderellas present an improvised scene showing how their plan has changed the story.

Adaptation
Older students may be asked to consider ways which will cross the cultural versions of the story.

Activity 2 Option 2: Exploring Character: The Hero — Prince

Tableaux
In groups, students explore the life of one prince. The prince and 4 or 5 other characters that are close to that prince (parent, messenger, aid to the prince, royal subject) work together.

The teacher can allocate stories to groups or let groups choose.

The students create a series of tableaux that show what life is like for a prince. Depending on language ability, these could move into **improvisation**.

Adaptation

The students present the biography of the Prince. They prepare this as a television production for the "Biography channel". (Scenes from the Prince's past and present life can be portrayed in the background as the Prince himself is interviewed by a T.V. host.)

The Royal Policy

In groups of 4–5, students work with different stories. Each group is formed of a prince and his government officials. In role, each group makes a list of important notes about the royal kingdom. Each group discusses what important things need to happen to bring the kingdom into this century.

Writing

Write the Royal Policy implementing all important issues required to help them bring the kingdom up to date. Beginners: write the policy in list form.

Note: with younger students the class can work with one or fewer stories.

Adaptation

Older/Intermediate/Advanced

Each group of Prince and officials take it in turns to present their policy at an official reading in the Royal Court (formed of other class members).

Post-Drama

Writing

Option One: Cinderella writes her new story, which may be one presented in class or a combination of several.

Option Two: The students write the biography of the Prince.

Younger Students

The teacher can take snapshots of the tableau work during the session. Students then write a short story to accompany the photographs. This can be made into a booklet entitled *A Day In The Life Of A Prince,* for example.

Session B

Pre-Drama

Any pre-drama activity

Drama Session

Activity 1: Exploration of Magical Powers

Note: It is possible to explore either:

a) How the powers of magic in each story work together or

b) How the powers of magic from each story work independently.

a)   In the role of a magic power, students (SIR) introduce themselves at a magic convention and explain how they use their magic (the fairy godmother might want to advertise her general abilities, her ability to transform people's wardrobes from old and used to new and elegant, to create instant transportation for any occasion). There are many different forms of magic in other Cinderella versions that can be played with.

b)   Using one or several of the tales, SIR design one of the following in order to attract people to their services:
>   an advertisement for themselves to be published in a magazine/newspaper;
>   pamphlet,
>   booth at the fair;
>   something else of their choice.

Note: remind students the aim is to explore the powers of magic.

Adaptation

Discuss what makes a good advertisement, how to make it attractive, language used, etc.

c)   Invite one or two of the SIR from one or several of the tales to the class. They present their services. The class question them about their powers.

Post-Drama

Changing the Magic

Students take one of the stories and insert a different magic power of their choice. Students discuss how this would change the story.

Writing
Write the new story.

SESSION C

Props/Materials: Miscellaneous items of clothing, and/or paper/materials to create clothing.

PRE DRAMA

Pre drama activity

DRAMA SESSION

Cultural Fashion Show

Group formation activity (4–5 persons each group)

a) Students in each group take the role of Royal fashion designer, fashion consultants, Royal model, etc. Each group is assigned a story from a different country. **Students in role (SIR)**, in their group, discuss the fashion and clothing trends for their story.

b) Each group designs, makes and models the garments for their country. Students may want to update the garments but still keep the traditions of the country.

c) SIR prepare a description for their garments as they will be presented at a fashion show to the general Royal public, other fashion consultants, designers and the press.

Garments can be made by gathering miscellaneous clothing articles from home or by making them from tissue paper etc. The teacher should be resourceful in helping students gather materials.

d) (Optional) Garments are presented at the Royal fashion show.

SESSION D

In this session students link the tales to the cultures in which they are set and search for tales from different cultures.

Props/Materials: Maps and information on the different countries.
Young Students: Materials to make a mural.

Older Students: Materials to make an information booklet.

Exploring Cultural Settings

Students locate the various places of origin on a map and study its land, agriculture, industry, language, etc.

Younger students may need to work in their own language for this and may need help and guidance.

Adaptation
Younger Students
Mural: In groups, students compose mural of the setting of their story based on what they have discovered in their research and in the story itself. Students list words or phrases that describe the setting. These are printed onto the mural.

Related Writing
Working independently or in pairs, students write a brief description of the place to be included in a pamphlet for tourists who plan to visit.

Intermediate/Advanced
Each group writes a description/summary of the information found out about one of the countries, so that all countries are covered. This could take the form of an information booklet provided by the tourist board.

Finding Other Tales Across Cultures
Students research other tales across different cultures. They can choose/create their own drama activities for exploring a new tale.

POST-DRAMA

Writing General
In a journal entry, Cinderellas reflect on the moment they first laid eyes on their Prince. The stepsisters reflect in their journals the night of Cinderella's wedding. Write Cinderella's father's thoughts as his health fails and he sees his new wife's step-daughters' treatment of his daughter. Write a familiar tale from your native language. Rewrite one of the tales from the point of view of one of the other characters, one of the princes or the ugly sisters.

Intermediate/Advanced

Rewrite a tale, changing the characters or distorting the events (Cinderella doesn't have to be a person, Cinderella set in the future). Re-stage a familiar tale from your own language in a different cultural context. Write an essay on cultural difference.

LANGUAGE ABILITY TABLE

Dramatic Exploration of Story: Cinderella Across Cultures	Language Ability									Writing Ability						
	a	b	c	d	e	f	g	h	l	1	2	3	4	5	6	7
Familiarizing Participants with the Stories	▓		▓				▓									
Exploring Character: Cinderella	▓															
Exploring Character: Prince	▓													▓		
Royal Policy	▓					▓								▓		
Further Activities	▓												▓			
Exploration of Magical Powers	▓		▓										▓			
Cultural Fashion Show	▓					▓										
Exploring Cultural Settings	▓		▓													
Research	▓						▓									
Writing												▓		▓		

Language Ability		
A. Discussing	G. Specialized language	W.4. Formal writing
B. Vocabulary	H. Reading	W.5. Writing for the media
C. Listening	L. Literature link	W.6. Discursive essay
D. Speaking	W.1. Personal writing	W.7. Taking of notes
E. Description	W.2. Creative/imag. writing	
F. Part. Grammar points	W.3. Writing for publishing	

4.5 DELTA X

This drama unit takes students on a journey back in the past to look at an imaginary drug and examines its effect on different communities.

Format:	One introductory lesson followed by further activities which can be spread over one or various lessons.
Stimulus:	Problem posed **in mantle of the expert**.
Class Size:	10+ — excellent for large classes.
Props/Materials:	Oath of Allegiance and Secrecy (see appendix), government report on Delta X (see appendix); reports on drugs for group work (see appendix), newspaper report on Delta X (improvised or see appendix), phial or bottle of coloured liquid to symbolize Delta X, paper and coloured pens, bag of assorted articles: clothing, hats, miscellaneous objects.
Preparation:	Prepare documents above, review dramatic strategies.
Teacher's Role:	Stimulate, build belief etc.

PRE-DRAMA

Any non-language pre-drama activity

DRAMA SESSION

Activity 1: Mantle of the Expert

The **Teacher in role** (TIR) introduces herself as a Government representative and asks the students in role as expert scientists to sign an oath of secrecy and allegiance. She passes the document round and everyone signs it.

TIR improvises or reads out top secret preliminary report to scientists. The teacher divides the class into groups, making sure each group contains students with a range of language abilities. Each group is given different written reports on the drug Delta X: the drug that makes all your wishes come true.

In their groups the scientists study the written reports regarding the drug and prepare notes for an oral report to be read out to the other scientists by their spokesperson. They are, collectively, given the mission to find the five most dangerous consequences of using this drug. Each piece of information that they can share with their colleagues will help compile this list.

The teacher tries to keep out of the way, but maintains the TL rule.

TIR intervenes by informing scientists she has new information. She reads aloud (or improvises) a newspaper report by saying that news of Delta X has reached the press. Their job is now of utmost importance. The scientists are given a little longer to compile their reports, then in turn, each representative of each group presents their report to the other scientists.

The students, in role as scientists, discuss the dangers of drug in accordance with their findings.

The teacher keeps the discussion moving, makes sure main points are noted down and brings it to a close.

Activity 2: Ritual

A phial of coloured liquid is placed in the centre of the room and participants form a circle around it. The teacher explains that the liquid in the phial is Delta X.

Each person, including the teacher, has a piece of paper and coloured pens. The teacher explains that they are all in role as people in the land where Delta X is available and that they are to draw a picture of or write down what they would wish for if they could have a sip of the liquid. As each person finishes they go, in turn, into the circle and stand beside the phial and read aloud what they have written or explain their drawing. They then lay their paper beside the phial and return to their place in the circle. If students are hesitant the teacher begins.

The students reflect out of role as to what has been learned about the kingdom.

FURTHER DRAMA ACTIVITIES

Teachers can make this one lesson or spread the activities over various lessons. This will depend on the age and language ability of the students and the speed at which they work.

Activity 1: Planning the Mission

TIR as Government Representative explains to the students that she needs their help to go back into the past to find out how and why the drug was first made. Delta X is killing those who take it.

She needs volunteers to take the role of members of the research team.

Note: Keep this team relatively small.

The teacher encourages volunteers to come forward, or picks a team. The other participants become people who live on the island where Delta X is made. Each group is told its mission:

Research Team
- Create a time capsule (using props, paper and/or furniture).
- Create characters with purpose on mission (e.g. an archaeologist, a psychologist, a doctor, laboratory assistant ... etc).
- Prepare visit: aims, expectations etc.

Islanders
- In accordance with numbers, the participants create different groups of their choice whom the research team will meet. Each group must have something to do with Delta X, directly or indirectly (peasants growing the crop, shop selling Delta X, drug dealer selling drug to other islands, laboratory producing drug, bad witch, etc.).
- Create their own space on the island (can use props) in different parts of the room.
- Prepare a situation which the research team will walk into presenting an obstacle for them to overcome, in order to find out something new about Delta X. The groups can confer if they wish.

The teacher should keep a balance between (1) the time spent on this activity — leaving enough time for them to prepare and build belief in what they are doing and (2) the time left for the visit. If Activity 2 is to be continued in another lesson it should be possible to move/keep the time capsule and anything constructed as part of the island.

Activity 2: The Mission

The **Teacher in Role** as Government representative reminds the research team that they are going on a dangerous and important journey. **Thought Tracking**: as the teacher places her hand on their head, each member of the research team tells how he feels at this moment and what his objectives of the visit are.

The teacher (as teacher) then guides a series of short scenes enacting the visit to the island. Students may have prepared an order in which things are to happen, or each group may have a separate event/obstacle for the research team to overcome. The teacher explains that participants may have to improvise as the scenes progress in order to make each scene part of the same story and move the story along.

These can be covered in the same lesson or spread over various lessons.

Things our students did with this:

- The islanders set a trap to see what the research team would wish for. They informed the team that they took the drug all the time and it never hurt them.
- The laboratory that produced Delta X from the plants was run by an old scientist who held the formula in his head. He tests the scientists to see if they are really scientists. He wants to know what has been discovered in the future. He informs it is made from all natural ingredients and that the problem lies in the people who take the drug, not the composition of the drug itself.
- The good witch was waiting for the scientists, she saw the visit in her crystal ball. She told them the islanders who grew the crop took Delta X all the time but they only wished for good things. It never harmed them. The people from the future wished for bad things — greed, power — and that is why they died.

Activity 3: The Message

The research team sends a message or messages back to the people of the future. This can take any form (a dramatic presentation, a choral message, a simple verbal message from each of them or a spokesperson, a letter or e-mail, etc.).

Post-Drama

Writing

As an islander of your choice, write an entry in your diary re: visit of strangers. Newspaper report on Delta X, brochures either promoting or banning Delta X. Write a page in your diary in role as scientist before appearing on a live TV interview show to speak about Delta X. As a research team member, write your formal report on returning to the future. As an islander of your choice write a letter to the government of the future regarding Delta X and why it is important not to destroy it

Discursive Essays

Should drugs be made legal? How does modern society view drug taking? Drugs in the Twenty-First Century.

LANGUAGE ABILITY TABLE

Delta X: The Drug that Makes Your Wishes Come True	Language Ability									Writing Ability						
	a	b	c	d	e	f	g	h	l	1	2	3	4	5	6	7
Mantle of the Expert	▓		▓				▓									
Ritual			▓													▓
Planning the mission	▓															
The Mission			▓	▓												
The Message				▓	▓											
Follow Up Writing Projects										▓			▓	▓		

Language Ability		
A. Discussing	G. Specialized language	W.4. Formal writing
B. Vocabulary	H. Reading	W.5. Writing for the media
C. Listening	L. Literature link	W.6. Discursive essay
D. Speaking	W.1. Personal writing	W.7. Taking of notes
E. Description	W.2. Creative/imag. writing	
F. Part. Grammar points	W.3. Writing for publishing	

4.6 THE SIBYL

This unit uses an unfinished story to create an imaginary kingdom where moral choices have to be made. It is particularly suitable for long-term development. It has been used very successfully to run alongside both a whole term and a whole year's work by doing all of the further activities suggested at the end of each session.

Format: Four sessions A-D, with extensive post drama activities.

Time should be taken to build belief in the first two sessions and teachers should then decide how long they wish to spend on each following activity.

Stimulus: Unfinished story (see appendix).

Class Size: 10+: suitable for large classes.

Props/Materials: See each session separately.

Preparation: Encourage students to build belief and revise drama strategies.

Teacher's Role: Ensure continuity through a series of short dramatic activities, encourage participants to make decisions and move the drama forward, intervene in or out of role to help with language or drama development, decide when to stop sessions to maintain interest for next workshop.

SESSION A

Props/Materials

Story (see appendix): pasted or written on a scroll if possible. Statue inscription (optional): we wrote ours in indelible pen on a marble tile, but it could be on wood or stone, or even card. It could be in a nonsense language/code which the teacher helps the participants decipher or a language that one of the participants speaks or "pidgin English/Spanish/French", etc.

Articles to make map/model of kingdom, scissors, glue, pens, coloured paper, roll or large-sized paper for map, etc.

PRE-DRAMA

Any non-language pre-drama activity

DRAMA SESSION

Teacher's Introduction

Explain the use of the drama circle to participants who are unfamiliar with it.

Activity 1: Setting the Scene

The **Teacher in role** (TIR) as narrator begins:

> *Come and sit down and listen carefully. I am going to tell*
> *you a story from long, long ago and I need your help ....*

TIR reads the story of the Sibyl (see appendix) from the scroll. The students sit round the storyteller and listen to the story. After reading the story, the narrator tells her listeners:

> *I need you to help me discover what this story tells us*
> *about this land and its people. What is it that the king*
> *most values?*

Note: for students of a lower level or those unused to this way of working it will help for students to, in a drama circle re-cap/ discuss story to make sure they have understood and to highlight main points/characters. This is done by the teacher asking open questions: Who were the people in the story? What do we know about them? What do we know about the kingdom? What can you tell me about this kingdom? What does this tell us about the people?

The teacher then tells the participants they are entering the story before the last three scrolls have been presented to the king for the last time.

Activity 2: Building Belief — Inscription on Statue (optional)

In a drama circle, the teacher passes the inscription round or shows it to everyone. Participants translate the inscription and tell what new information it gives about the people and/or the land.

Adaptation

For beginners teachers could substitute a statue/figure and say it is a replica of one in the kingdom and ask the students what it shows them about the kingdom.

Activity 3: Statues

Group formation exercise to form groups of 2-5 people

Students are asked to use their bodies to create a group statue to be found in the kingdom. The statue should tell us something new or build upon something we know about the kingdom.

Examples from workshops we have given:

> Goddess of fertility offering her daughter to a god. the three
> scrolls, each indicating a subject contained in it by a figure

standing over it. The forces of nature: sun, sea, moon, which the people worshipped. Sibyl burning the scrolls by using lightning (magic).

Groups take it in turns to show their statue to the others who guess what the statue represents. Students are then asked what this statue tells us about the kingdom or its people.

Activity 4: Building Belief — Map or Model of Kingdom

Group formation exercise (class divided into 2)

Each group makes a map or model of the kingdom showing what it is we have learned so far and adding/showing three new things about the kingdom or its inhabitants.

This usually turns out to be a 3D map. When possible, participants should work in the TL.

Note: This exercise should be included whatever the age of the participants.

Groups are asked to examine the map/model made by the opposite team.

Writing

Working with the map/model from the opposite group, groups write down:

a)   Three adjectives that describe the kingdom as portrayed by the opposite group.

b)   Three adjectives about the way they feel when they look at the map (curious, dreamy, angry ...)

c)   Three things which are different/new about this map/model.

Do not ask for sentences, just the words that come to mind. Keep the focus at this point, away from grammar. This exercise can be tailored to the language level of the class in question.

Groups share findings and come to a consensus, if necessary by voting, as to which new things remain in the story (a particular lay-out of mountain, cave and castle; a new character).

SESSION B

Props/Materials

Map/models of kingdom made last session. Scrolls, teacher makes scrolls to look old and authentic, with parts of text that will test the participants but which they will also be able to understand/or guess the meaning of. These pieces of text will tell the readers something about the unknown kingdom. Objects from the kingdom (a coin, a pebble, an item of jewellery).

PRE-DRAMA

Pre-drama game, movement based.

DRAMA SESSION

Map/models are put in a place of prominence in the room.

Teacher's Introduction: The teacher quickly recaps what happened last session and what it is that everyone found out about the kingdom. The teacher explains that the job today is to investigate the kingdom.

Group Formation Exercise: Groups of 2–8, depending on the size of the class. Suggestion: word association (see 7.2) using words from the final exercise, last lesson.

Activity 1: Still Images — Group Decision Making

The teacher says she knows there are problems in this kingdom as in any land. Each group is asked to create its own group still image of a problem in the country.

Each image is presented to the other participants and its implications are noted. (Image of the king being pulled in two directions shows he is indecisive, king pointing his finger at a wronged subject shows he is unjust — etc.).

Adaptation
With younger groups a list could be made of things learned so far (on the blackboard or on a big sheet of paper put up on the wall) which could be kept for use in further sessions. Students could add to this themselves or a **scribe** could be allocated.

Group Formation Exercise: Groups of 2–5

Activity 2: Mantle of the Expert

The teacher gives each group an artefact(s) and a scroll. The students are told that they are esteemed archaeologists who have come together for a conference to present their findings regarding

• the scroll they are given;
• the artefact(s) they are given.

The students **in role** as architects are asked by the teacher (in role as convenor of conference) to:

1. give themselves and their group of archaeologists a name;
2. decide in their groups whether the objects they have been given are a part of the kingdom or not;
3. prepare a written report (or notes to be read out) to be presented to the rest of the conference members.

Whilst the participants are working on their objects and preparing reports, the teacher sets up the room as for a conference meeting. The teacher also provides support to the participants in the way of helping with vocabulary, etc., if required, and enforces the TL rule.

The teacher allocates the order in which groups are to appear. She finds out the name of the first group's presenter and asks each group to find out from the group which is to follow them:

• the name of their group;
• where they are from;
• the name of their presenter.

This means they can introduce this group at the end of their own presentation.

The teacher takes the role of Convenor, introduces the first group and lets the conference roll.

The teacher keeps things moving and acts as chairperson.

Out of role, in the **drama circle**, the participants discuss what they have learned about the kingdom, adding to the list of things learned, if kept.

Adaptation

In the case of beginners the teacher may like to include more information in the materials provided. Students can present findings as a group rather than making one person spokesperson. The teacher may permit the use of dictionaries or go around and help groups in problems. Lower-level students could be allowed to work in their own language(s) whilst deciphering scrolls as long as their report/talk is given in the TL.

SESSION C

Props/Materials

Maps/models of kingdom, scrolls and objects from the kingdom that were accepted in last class, atmospheric music (optional), lights for atmosphere (optional), **puzzle poetry** cards, additional sheets of paper and pens for Activity 3.

PRE-DRAMA

Any movement-based pre-drama activity.

DRAMA SESSION

Teacher's introduction: The teacher **in role** as narrator reminds the students of the details/description of the kingdom that they invented last session.

The teacher explains that the job today is to find out what it is that the king most valued.

Activity 1: Hotseating of Characters

Students and teacher (as participant and not as teacher) ask questions of characters who will give us some insight on the king (someone who knows the king, or who has overheard the king/seen him do something, who can tell the group something about the king).

The teacher explains to the students that the idea is to build upon the story so far. The character may or may not want to answer, but the drama has to move forward, so some answers have to be given.

Note: We usually start by leaving the hotseat free and substituting a visual image for the person (see glossary). E.g., a feather duster for the maid, a scroll for the Sibyl. Later someone could take the hotseat. If students want to speak to the king this is at the teacher's discretion, but they may NOT ask him the direct question what it is that he most values.

Activity 2: Evoking Emotion

The lights are turned down and perhaps eerie music is played. Participants say aloud negative adjectives that come to mind when they think of the king or his kingdom.

The lights are turned up or perhaps fairy lights are used / happy music played and participants give positive reactions to the king or his kingdom.

Teacher or student acting as **scribe** takes down words.

Activity 3: Puzzle Poetry

Divide the class into two: using words given in the last exercise, the teacher whispers negative words to half the class, positive to the other. Students say the words to one another to find positive and negative groups.

The groups are told that in order to find out more about the king they will be exploring JOY (positive group) and FEAR (negative group) in the kingdom.

The teacher places words on the floor. The groups collect words and form a piece of prose or poetry on the floor from these together with any of the words they were given in the group formation exercise The teacher provides sheets of paper for these words to be written on and inserted if required. This prose/poetry must express positive /negative feelings about the king or any of his actions which may have arisen as a result of the hotseating.

The teacher may help students if necessary. Remember to enforce the TL rule.

Groups are invited to present the poetry/prose in a dramatised manner (choral/line or word per person/swaying/with music/song etc)

Activity 4: Teacher in Role (Optional)

If ideas are needed for the drama or the drama needs moving on.

The teacher takes the role of the Sibyl sitting in her cave. She invites participants, in role as the villagers to come and visit. She makes them aware that they have come to ask her not to burn the last three scrolls. She invites them to talk to her about who they are and what they feel. She answers in riddles or veiled messages which also tell something about the king. Students then have to make sense of what she says.

SESSION D

Props/Materials

Maps/models of kingdom, scrolls and objects from the kingdom that were accepted by the archaeologists, three blank scrolls (in case scroll writing exercise is inserted).

PRE DRAMA

Any movement — based pre-drama activity

DRAMA SESSION

Group formation — class divided into three.

Activity 1: What Does the King Value? In the Style of

Each group is to present a scene which shows what it is that the king most values. Each group is given a different format in which to present. The styles are a T.V. report, pop video and flashbacks/ flashforwards. Groups are encouraged to be as creative as they like (from our students: youth, children, money, his kingdom, his throne, family).

If all groups give the same answer (highly unlikely) omit follow-ing exercise and choose an activity from further activities, for ex-ample writing the content of the scrolls.

Activity 2: Signing the Space

Group Formation Exercise: The teacher takes the two or three different things that the king most values and moves around the room whispering one to each person in turn so that two/three new groups are formed.

Each group is asked to (1) form the Sibyl's cave, or a scene in the cave to (2) prove or disprove whether or not the king most values the thing they have been given. The groups can use objects or drawings or documents to leave a trail.

The students then go to the other groups' caves and find out which of the things they have been representing and whether it is true or not.

Activity 3: Decision Making

Situation One: If only one cave says YES
The session is finished or the teacher may choose to do an activity from the Post-Drama section.

Situation Two: If all or two of the caves say YES
Either:
• The students elect someone as the decision maker. The other students make either a corridor of voices which shout out what the king most values as the decision maker walks through or they become voices in the head of the decision maker. The decision maker decides which thing it is the king most values;

OR

- The class forms a circle. The participants are told that one (or two) of the caves are fake and the group comes to a consensus as to which cave is the real one.

Situation Three: If all of the caves say NO:
The class forms a circle. The students are told that two of the caves are fake and the group comes to a consensus as to which cave is the real one.

The students are then given writing assignments to complete — see Post-Drama

POST DRAMA

These activities can be used in further sessions, to extend the session above, or develop into a class project.

Writing
Write the content of the scrolls.

a)   Each person can be asked to write one entry on the scroll – for example pass the scroll round the circle. Participants can then collaborate in order to create three scrolls.
b)   Each scroll can be seen to have a theme and class is divided into groups and each group writes a scroll

Remember to remain faithful to the drama. Students may need to include some of the contents of the scrolls they have accepted as part of the kingdom if these have been seen to relate to the Sibyl's scrolls.

Class writing project: The Kingdom's Newspaper.

The whole newspaper can be written, including the editorial on the penultimate (next to last) visit of the Sibyl.

a)   This exercise could be dramatized with reporters visiting students in role as characters; or
b)   Students could work in groups, each on a section of the newspaper: editorial, front page article, other articles, advertisements, obituaries, etc. This can be channelled to the language level of the students and include drawings for the younger students.
c)   This exercise could be changed to articles for a sensationalist newspaper and a serious newspaper and the two compared, especially if the students are studying the media in class.

Personal Writing: The entry in the King's diary the night before the Sibyl comes for the last time.

Discursive Essay: This could be tailored to match a theme being discussed in class, such as Power or Fame and Fortune.

Drama

Group Improvisation, Forum Theatre (the subject will depend on what the class has given you as teacher to work with/build upon).

Choose one key scene, or get participants to choose from, for example:

* the king the night before the sibyl comes;
* the king's last meeting with his counsellors;
* visit of villagers to king the night before the Sibyl comes;
* riot by villagers before Sibyl comes;
* last visit of Sibyl to King.

These, or other situations will appear in the course of the things the participants have brought up over the two sessions.

One group improvises the scene. Others then add their ways of seeing things by taking the place of one of the characters and re-enacting with a different outcome (see forum).

LANGUAGE ABILITY TABLE

The Sibyl	Language Ability									Writing Ability						
	a	b	c	d	e	f	g	h	l	1	2	3	4	5	6	7
Teacher's Introduction			■													
Setting the Scene				■												
Discussion	■															
Building Belief	■		■	■			■									
Statues	■															
Writing		■				■										■
Teacher's Introduction																
Tableaux	■					■										■
Mantle of the Expert	■			■	■											
Teacher's Introduction				■												
Hotseating of Characters		■		■												
Evoking Emotion				■												■
Puzzle Poetry		■											■			
Teacher in Role			■	■												
In the Style of	■					■										
Signing the Space	■	■									■	■	■			
Decision Making	■												■	■		
Further Activities										■			■			

Language Ability		
A. Discussing	G. Specialized language	W.4. Formal writing
B. Vocabulary	H. Reading	W.5. Writing for the media
C. Listening	L. Literature link	W.6. Discursive essay
D. Speaking	W.1. Personal writing	W.7. Taking of notes
E. Description	W.2. Creative/imag. writing	
F. Part. Grammar points	W.3. Writing for publishing	

PRE-DRAMA ACTIVITIES

5. I MOVEMENT GAMES

Untangle the Circle

Everyone forms a circle holding hands. One person is chosen to let go. They are now the first person. The first person leads the chain, going under arches made of arms and stepping over arms to form a muddle. No-one must let go of a hand. At the end the first person reaches the last person. They turn round and face the other way, joining the opposite hand to the hand they were holding and joining up with the spare hand. The group then have to untangle themselves to form a circle facing the same way again without letting go of hands. It can always be done. Instructions to one another should be given in the TL.

Simon Says....

The old children's party game. Teacher leads — Simon says ... touch your toes, Simon says ... clean you teeth.. Simon says... sit down.. Simon says hop around the room... Every time the teacher says "Simon says" followed by an action the students have to do it. At one point the teacher says an action without saying the words "Simon says" like "Stand up". If they do not hear "Simon says" then the students are NOT to perform the action. Anyone who does so is eliminated from the game. It makes it more difficult for the students if the teacher speeds up the instructions.

The aim of the teacher is to get the students to move about.

5.2 MIME

Difficulties With Objects

Someone mimes having problems with a large or small object in a particular situation (these can be given to the students by the teacher, or the students can invent their own). Other students guess what is happening (threading a needle on horseback, trying to get your money out of your purse for the toll whilst driving and answering your mobile phone, putting on a pair of shoes that are too small for you).

Mirroring Exercises

In pairs or as a whole group one person or everyone copies/mirrors what someone else is doing. In pairs one person mimes an action or moves his arm up, the other person follows with the opposite arm as if he is the mirror image; or one person leads the whole class in a line. He walks on his toes, everyone walks on their toes, he crawls on the floor, everyone crawls on the floor.

A Piece of Putty

Students Sit in a circle — they throw an imaginary piece of putty to one another and each person pretends to shape/fashion it into an object. The others guess what it is.

5.3 LANGUAGE GAMES

Objects

Everyone is blindfolded. Someone is given an object that they can only feel. They have to describe it and everyone else guesses what it is.

Alien to Earthman

Alien describes an object to the Earthman by size, shape, colour, feel etc. The Earth people have to guess what it is.

Emotions

A situation is given by the teacher (job interview, meeting with the headmaster, proposal of marriage). In pairs people are asked to act out the situation in the style of the emotion given by the teacher (angrily, enthusiastically, sleepily, ecstatically, etc.).

Note: it helps if the teacher gives the same situation and emotion to the whole class, and changes the emotion from time to time.

Making Sense of Sentences

This exercise involves "playing with language". It helps teach the basic elements of sentence structure AND the rhythms and inflections of different pieces of text.

Working as a Large Group

The group stands in a circle. The teacher chooses an unfamiliar sentence which matches the group's language abilities (this may be chosen from a prose source eg., a newspaper article or a poetic passage from a play like a soliloquy). The group speaks the sentence as a CHORUS until they get a sense of the rhythm of the piece.

Each student is then given one word to speak. The students speaking one word at a time try to speak the passage as if it was one person speaking 'naturally'.

Variations

- Cut well known sentences or everyday expressions into one word pieces. Divide class into small groups so that number in each group fits the number of words in the sentence. Encourage each student to say the words randomly. Encourage each student to say the words randomly while at the same time moving around the room. Teachers can vary this by asking them to run or skip or crawl along the floor.

- Present small groups of students with single words from a sentence with which they are unfamiliar. Ask them to speak the words until they think the words are in the right order. Ask them to speak the words in a group AS IF the group is a single person (placing the stress and inflections in the right places in the sentence).

- For 'beginners' as for the previous variation but colour code the sentences using different colours for each element of the sentence (verb, subject, object, adverb) to help students know which word should be where.

- Mix up the groups so that now each group has words from several different sentences. Encourage students to find different ways of arranging the sentences to make 'sense'/to create poetic images.

5.4 BASIC BREATH AND VOICE WORK

Vocal Warm-up Using Adjectives

Students form a circle, standing or sitting. In turn they voice the following — quietly and loudly and expressively: It is quiet, so quiet, IT IS LOUD SO LOUD, it is quiet so quiet, IT IS LOUD SO LOUD. The different sounds should reverberate round the circle.

The teacher can vary the adjectives: I am happy/sad, it is dark/ light, it is high/low, etc.

Vocal Warm-up Using Poetry

Class read a poem with vivid sounds as a group chorus, or in groups. (e.g., Bleezer's Ice Cream) as a group chorus, or in groups. *We suggest "Bleezer's Ice Cream" by Jack Prelutsky or "Night is Come" by Sir Henry Newbold, both to be found in Booth and Moore (1988)*

Finding the "WU CHI POSITION" — Relaxed Tension

Teacher guides the following easy movements:

a) stand feet no more than hip width apart with OUTSIDE edges of feet parallel to one another (you may feel SLIGHTLY knock-kneed) and with your knees slightly bent.

b) imagine a string attached that pulls you up from the head and a string at the tailbone that pulls you down, like a ballet dancer.

c) imagine your head back on a pillow, don't lean forward, knees slightly bent. Relax chin down but keep eyes parallel to the floor.

d) tuck the duck ... gently tilt the pelvic girdle under so as to help straighten spinal column and lose "duck tail".

e) keep spine straight but not rigid! (Imagine an equal cushion of air between each vertebra which are parallel with each other.)

f) shrink hip carriage (bottom moves back so that chest appears to move forward — so that if a jewel were hung around your neck it would fall right between your feet).

g) keep feet parallel, teeth lightly touching, lips softly closed, tongue should rest on top of the palate close to the teeth.

h) hands relaxed by sides, fingers pointing towards the ground.

Finding the Heart of Breath

a) Stand in Wu Chi position.

b) Form a heart-shape with hands, keeping shoulders rounded, place the thumbs just above the belly button and the tips of fingers on the pubic bone.

c) Drop elbows/ relax shoulders.

d) Breathe in through the nose and down to the heart-shaped area, breathe slowly, smoothly, and fluidly, do **NOT** hold or force your breathing.

e) As you breathe in imagine balloons filling up between and behind knees, under arms.

f) As you breathe out allow tension to flow out with the breath.

CAUTION: *if you know you are pregnant or you are menstruating or have an ulcer you should breathe above the top of your thumbs. When speaking try to breathe into heart of breath unless otherwise stated.*

Voice/Gesture/Breath in WU CHI Stance
(Breath and Sound Warm-Up)

a) Start in WU CHI position. As you breathe in, imagine breath to be very expensive vintage wine; taste the air in your mouth, drink it, relax, keep in alignment;

b) Imagine air as a piece of food (eg.,Belgian chocolate); take air in and chew; alternate between drinking and chewing the air;

c) Yawn and sigh; drop jaw and let the air out; drink and chew the air and yawn; feel the impulse in the body that the yawn is coming from; allow arms to follow the yawn (don't force it) but allow sound to increase with the yawn.

d) Centre your breathing again; hum softly and gently until you feel a tingle as you hum; let hands drop, open elbows, lift up your arms so that your palms are at about heart height facing your body. Imagine you are hugging a medium sized tree, think of yourself as firm on the outside & soft on the inside, focus on the column of air, empty between.

e) Find your resonating point; the body is full of resonators which can be used when talking or singing. Resume "the hug tree" stance. SMILE! (it helps); gently hum. Imagine you have a balloon between your arms. As you breathe in, imagine filling the balloon with energy.

5.5 MOVEMENTS WITH SOUND

Frisbee

Stand in WU CHI position. Imagine you have a frisbee in each hand. Using basic sounds, Mmm, Aaah, Eye, Eee, Rrrh, Oooo, Lll, Nng. Play frisbee with each sound. Play with pitch and volumes of sounds as you move your hands as if playing Frisbee.

Note to teacher: this is best done with all the class playing frisbee at the same time.

Circle

Imagine you see something that really excites you in the middle of the circle and pick it up, use sound to express joy/excitement. Put object down, walk, stop, back to hum (mmm).

Play the Accordion

Raise hands so that palms face belly button. Imagine you are lightly holding an English concertina (or similar small accordion). Start by simply HUMMING softly. Now start to move your hands away from one another as if playing an accordion. Release sounds when arms extend out.

5.6 BASIC BODY MOVEMENTS

"Knocking at the Gates of Life"

a) Stand in the WU CHI position.
b) Place one arm at front and one arm at back
c) Movement is generated from centre of body
d) Arms follow hip movement,
e) Arms have a gentle swinging motion
f) Arms gently strike belly button and point where spine connects to hips
g) Don't hit kidneys

"Rotating the Dragons Pearl"

a) Movement occurs from the central area, hip carriage.
b) Keep legs straight but do not lock knees.
c) Open arms, elbows out, imagine you are carrying a large ball or balloon between your palms.
d) Elbows and shoulders relaxed.
e) Move from the waist lead with belly button.
f) Hold and turn ball as you turn at waist, carry from side to side.
g) As waist moves rotate hands so that alternately the left and then the right hand is on top.
h) Breathe in as you turn waist to each side and rotate ball so that one palm faces up to sky and the other to the earth.
i) Breathe out as you return to centre and with palms facing towards the body.

Painting With Your Feet

Tell students to imagine their feet are paintbrushes and the floor is a large empty canvas. Tell them to create simple visual designs, to imagine what colour they will use on their brushes and to explore making light and heavy brush strokes.

Then ask them to explore making straight lines and angular turns on the canvas. Ask them to explore making circles, spirals and smooth turns on the canvas

Now Add Music

Tell students to simply move to the music. Change the colour of paint and the patterns they want to make.

Use a wide variety of music stimuli (Celtic, Classical, Rock, Rap, Ethnic, Country). Ask students to record comments (about patterns, weight, height, direction, speed), colours, sensations, feelings, etc.) after each piece of music is presented.

5.7 CHARACTER WORK

Walk My Walk

Partner A observes partner B's walk. Partner A places hand on partner B's shoulder and walks alongside them. Partner A walks AS IF they are Partner B.

Partner A (now moving as B) finds a new partner C who is moving as their former partner D. Following the steps above A walking as B takes on D's walk as conveyed by C.

Laban Working Story

Partner A walks away from partner C in character (i.e., as D). As their new character they climb stairs, open door, move heavy box (push along floor), (using a small, light paint brush) touch up paint on a window sill, wring out clothing, change quickly to meet beloved, run downstairs and out the door, struggle through tall grass & mud swatting mosquitoes as they go, meet beloved, ice skate, fight vending machine for a drink of pop, walk with beloved, say goodbye, go home...

At the end of this exercise make sure that all students return to being THEMSELVES by asking them to recite name, birth date, other significant personal information, etc. to themselves as they slowly return to their normal walk.

GROUP FORMATION EXERCISES

The following are examples of group formation exercises teachers may like to use. Teachers and students are also able to make up their own. Consult our bibliography for references of books which have good sections on the subject.

6.1 PAIRS

- Stand beside some who ... has the same colour socks... sits on the opposite side of the room...
- Split exchanges
    - Divide newspaper headlines into two. Give half to each person. Students walk around the room and repeat their part of the headline to as many people as possible until they find their pair, or as many pairs as is possible (e.g. British star/accused of Espionage (see Maley and Duff p. 106–8 for good ideas)).

    Note: If all students submit one headline teacher will have a list of sources.

    - Use grammar to divide exchanges, Can I sit here? ... Of course you can; What time is it? ... Half-past nine; When did it happen? ... At nine o'clock; Is it raining? ... Yes it is.
    - Use first and second lines of well known songs — in their own or the TL (tailor to class). (I'm singing in the rain — Just singing in the rain...; I just called, to say I love you — I just called to say how much I care, etc.).
    - (Advanced — larger groups) Use lines of poems they have studied.
- Students move about the room in some fashion: hopping on one foot, walking backwards, crawling, etc. When the teacher calls

freeze, students stand next to the person nearest to them. (Make sure students move around and don't hang near their friends).

- Divide the class in half and form two circles one inside the other. The inside circle moves to the right and outside circle move to the left. When teacher calls freeze, students pair up with the person they are facing.

- Half of the class are given cards with actions on. One student must find their partner by searching for the person who is miming the action on their card.

6.2 GROUPS

1. Animal Noises
   People are given the name of an animal on a sheet of paper. They have to make the noise until they find someone else/ others who make the same noise. (This could also be used with methods of transport: trains, cars, donkey,. aeroplane; or with sports — students imitating practising a sport.)

2. Word Association
   The opportunities are endless. Give each person a word on a piece of paper. Each person goes round and shares their word with someone else in the room. People have to guess the association of the words to form into groups. For example:

   Opposites — to divide class into pairs
   Happy/sad, black/white, heads/tails.

   Big/small, loud/quiet — class into two
   Nouns relating to very big things and nouns relating to very small things; or words relating to quiet things/noises or loud things/noises

   Animal/Vegetable/Mineral — class into three
   Nouns which are animal, vegetable or mineral.

   Rhyming — smaller groups
   People find words that rhyme with theirs
   Theirs; stairs; mares; cares
   Fear, near, beer, clear etc

3. Students move about the room (encourage students to use their space). Teacher calls out a number and the class forms that group number with the students nearest to them.

4. Find someone in the class that has the same number of syllables in their first name.

5. Hula hoops (large plastic hoops which are balanced around your middle as you circle your hips) or pieces cloth/ paper are placed on the floor. The students move about. When the teacher shouts a number, the same number of people have to jump in the hoop or stand on the cloth/paper.

6. All students wearing stripes, buttons, sweaters, skirts, shorts gather together. N.B. this may make odd numbered groups.

6.3 ADAPTING ACTIVITIES AND TEMPLATES

This section refers to sections 3 and 4 on how templates and activities can be made to fit particular classrooms. It takes the main points made therein and gives examples with reference to four templates:

- Old Age (referenced as OA)
- Quest (referenced as Qu)
- Weather (referenced as W)
- Cinderella (referenced as Cind)

Activities within the templates are referenced as follows:
Activity 1 = Act.1; Session B = Sess. B; so Session A
Activity 3 will be referenced as Sess. A, Act.3
Two activities in the same template in the same session, e.g. Activity 1 and Activity 3 will be written as Act1,3.

LANGUAGE ABILITIES

Beginner
OA: Act.1 — Instead of having a discussion, beginners give adjectives to describe the people in the pictures; this not only builds confidence but provides vocabulary for the session to follow.

Intermediate
OA: Post-Drama work: Intermediate students interview instead of describing; this involves question/answer, something all students within this bracket can handle confidently, using different structures according to their particular abilities. You can always ask more of them (by asking them to change the interview into reported speech).

Advanced
OA: Act.6:Adaptation: the making of comparisons gives students free space to write unguided, fluent prose.

TECHNIQUES FOR ADAPTING ACTIVITIES FOR DIFFERENT LANGUAGE ABILITIES

Instructions as to how to adapt a template sometimes occur within the template, see: W: Sess A. Act.1, 2 ;4. Sess B. Act.3; or Cind: Option 2. Act 2.

The teacher may however need to adapt activities where not indicated. In this case, certain techniques are useful:

Take a Role: OA: Act.4

In the overheard conversations activity the teacher can take a role to help in various ways: if the storyline is not progressing, if she wants to slant the story in a particular direction or add in a particular complication, if the students are shy, if she wants to introduce a certain kind of language work, if the students are not good orally, etc.

Set the Type of Language Used Orally: OA: Act.5

In this interview activity the reporters could be given set topics to investigate which would lead the language in a certain direction.

Note: Teacher can give the example and set the tense. This can be made very simple or quite complicated, depending on the type of question and the tenses used.

Qu: Act.6. In thought tracking it is the teacher who asks the questions and thus solicits an answer in a particular tense.

W. Sess.B. Act.1. When starting students off with storytelling, the teacher by giving an example, or by starting the story, already sets the tense and register of the story

Set the Type of Language Used by Introducing Information

W: Sess. A. Act.2.: By reading out or showing news headlines a certain type of language is given to the students, which they then follow. By then reading a report the whole tone and register is set for students to follow. You can therefore give very simple or highly complicated information in accordance with the language abilities of the students.

Use Different Dramatic Strategies to Match Language Ability

Qu: Act 5; Here the teacher is given various options to choose from in order to coincide with the ability of her classroom.

Cind Option 2. Act 1. With beginners tableaux are a good way to create a storyline and practise with drama without requiring speaking. The teacher can move into improvisation if the students are able to do this. If they are unable to improvise both verbally or dramatically she can move into the next activity or introduce other ways of going forward, such as asking one group to mime and the others to provide the words. In this way students have only one thing to think about (speaking or moving) rather than two.

Use Open Dramatic Activities
Qu: Act 5; Open drama activities allow students to take the drama off in the direction they choose or in the direction the teacher leads. They also allow the teacher to set the language in accordance with the ideas above.

OA: Act 5; by giving the students the opportunity to ask questions and invent answers, in pairs, without the class listening, the drama can move forward rapidly and in many different directions. This gives you different options to choose from when you decide together as a class how to move the drama forward.

Keep a List of Recurring Vocabulary/Important Points
Either do this on a large piece of card or on the board if there is one, so that everyone can see.

OA: Act4; It is helpful when a story is being developed to note down the important points so that they can all be built into the story and the teacher does not waste precious time recapping to make sure everyone has remembered everything. It also helps her to highlight important points by summarizing what is written down.

Qu: Act.6; When several drama activities or scenes in one activity follow one another in a short time there is often a lot of material produced that it is impossible to remember or recall in detail later if it is not taken down at the time.

W.Sess. A.Act.1,4. You can use an active listening ability to work with language at any level, and in each case it may be helpful to record the students' responses so that they can be worked with at whichever level and in whatever depth you ascertain. During drama work students often give vocabulary/phrase which is useful to recall and/or use later, so the compiling of a list helps teachers to build a resource to be used in whichever way she deems necessary or desirable; she can also give the job of the list making to a scribe to introduce writing or to give a job to a disruptive student and keep them occupied; or give the job to a student who is less mobile, more inhibited, or better at written than oral work.

Allow Real Beginners to Use a Dictionary
For example, W: Sess A. Act.4.

Life Experiences

Students of Different Ages

W and Cind: Both contain numerous examples of tasks that will involve the very young, the adolescent and the adult.

OA: Act.4: In an exercise such as overheard conversations, there will be very different content in the conversations of different age groups.

Qu: Act.5: Different age groups will connect this activity to their own interests.

W: Sess. B. Act.1. Discussions can go any way the students want, therefore in accordance with their own interests and life experiences.

Different age groups' reaction to parts of the drama can be compared both during and after the session itself.:

OA, Post Drama Time line: young students could do the end of the person's life and the older students the younger part of his life or v.v. In the essay writing about "what it is like to become old" students could compare the essays of different ages and what it is they see as becoming "old".

Cind. Sess A.Option 1. Act.1. Groups could be formed of different ages and their reactions compared.

Cind Sess A. Option 2. Act 2. The Policy from the view of different age groups could be compared. Different ages may or may not have different priorities.

Qu: the editorials of different age groups can be compared, etc.

Students From Different Cultures

Both the Quest and Cinderella are examples of group improvised dramas, which allow the teacher a lot of room to adapt activities to suit different cultures.

In OA Act.3. anyone can make something out of a piece of string, everyone is included in the activity and very little movement is required; in Act.4. the conversations are the people's own and interviews involve little movement/touching.

Living and Surrounding Environment

Qu: Offers suggestions for adaptations by using a story that is familiar or known making it more relevant to the group. This may include a story, tale, myth, or legend that is common to the region in which the students live; or it may be a selection from another area of the curriculum which speaks to the experiences of the group of students involved.

W: Works with students' own stories related to weather.
Cind: Works with everyday problems occurring in different cultures
OA: Requires personal input into what it means to grow older.

Bringing in Other Curriculum Areas
Cind: Sess B. Act.1. The elaboration of the advertisements could be linked to an art class or a computer class.
Cind. Post-Drama Research could be part of a geography class.
W: the music in Act.1. could be tailored to the group and the soundscape in act.4. linked to a music class.

We hope that these examples will give you ideas of how to personalize the templates to meet the requirements of your individual classroom. Please also refer to the section on language themes.

AT-A-GLANCE GUIDE
TO LANGUAGE

In this section we give you two different reference points to help select the templates for your language classes. For those of you interested in covering specific types of language work, we have devised a matrix which enables you to see at a glance which language abilities are covered in each template. At the end of each template you will find a more detailed table which shows which language ability is practised in each drama activity. For others who work with a language book divided into set topics we have a table which plots the themes covered in each template.

7. I LANGUAGE ABILITIES ASSOCIATED WITH TEMPLATES

We have divided language abilities into broad categories for ease of reference. They are denoted by letters as explained below. The same system is used in the tables at the end of each template.

A. Discussing
- negotiating (agreeing/disagreeing/persuading)
- forming questions/appropriate answers
- arguing a case
- reasoning/decision making
- planning
- summary

B. Vocabulary
- emotions/feelings
- physical characteristics

- movement
- animal sounds/groups, etc.

C. Listening
- listening comprehension
- dictation

D. Speaking
- improvised dialogue/narration
- presentation
- oral storytelling
- interview
- reading aloud

E. Description
- summary
- descriptive storytelling
- describing

F. Particular Grammar Points
- tenses
- sentences
- captions
- cloze
- comparisons
- conditionals
- adjectives, etc.

G. Specialized Language
- language of the press
- poetry
- opening lines of narrative
- language of advertisements
- titles

H. Reading

L. Literature Link

W. Writing

W.1. Personal Writing
- personal letter writing
- journal writing/diary entry
- postcard

W.2. Creative/imaginative Writing
- narrative: storytelling/ finish the story
- poetry
- description
- dialogue

W.3. Writing for Publishing
- script-writing
- book
- memoirs
- biography

W.4. Formal Writing
- formal letter writing
- formal report for presentation
- petition
- interview
- summary, synopsis
- formal log book

W.5. Writing for the Media
- newspaper reports/ articles
- editorials
- TV/ radio reports
- personal ad/ obituary
- pamphlet / informative booklet
- fashion report
- bumper sticker
- poster/advertisement

W.6. Discursive Essay

W.7. Taking of Notes
- jotting down ideas
- descriptive notes

7.2 LANGUAGE ABILITIES MATRIX

Template/Section	Language Ability									Writing Ability						
	a	b	c	d	e	f	g	h	l	1	2	3	4	5	6	7
The Shopping Mall	■		■		■	■	■				■			■		
Memories	■	■	■					■			■					
Old Age		■	■	■				■								
Building One Minute Stories	■	■	■	■	■			■								
Nursery Rhymes	■							■					■			
The Lion's Den	■	■						■			■	■				
Abstract Art	■															
Dramatic Approaches To Telling Story	■	■														
Communication Is The Key										■	■	■				
Trapped Behind Enemy Lines	■	■					■	■		■						
My Grandfather	■	■														
Emigration				■				■		■						
The Quest				■						■						■
Weather							■			■						■
Missing Persons	■						■				■					■
There Are Two Sides to Every Story	■	■			■	■				■						
Cinderella Across Cultures	■			■			■			■						
Delta X		■		■		■		■		■						
The Sibyl	■	■	■	■	■		■			■						■

Language Ability		
A. Discussing	G. Specialized language	W.4. Formal writing
B. Vocabulary	H. Reading	W.5. Writing for the media
C. Listening	L. Literature link	W.6. Discursive essay
D. Speaking	W.1. Personal writing	W.7. Taking of notes
E. Description	W.2. Creative/imag. writing	
F. Part. Grammar points	W.3. Writing for publishing	

7.3 LANGUAGE TOPICS MATRIX

Many of you who teach a language as a foreign language will be assigned a set book to follow throughout the year in order to comply with curriculum requirements. Whichever theoretical standpoint this book takes it will, most probably, be divided into broad themes or topics based units such as Parents and Children, The Daily News, Equality of Opportunity etc. Each unit will be divided into divisions such as reading and discussion material, grammar and lexis, listening, writing strategies, appropriacy and register, etc. For those of you who need to follow this system, we have devised a table which shows you, at a glance, which templates can be linked to which topics, so that the drama session can be used alongside themes studied in the language classroom.

Should you be required to deal with a set topic, you will be able to slant the events in the drama to cover it. For example in Old Age you could slant the focus toward at least four different topics:

Parents and Children: Beginning with the pre-language drama activity, students are asked to think about their own grandparents. In creating the storyline from the string the teacher can slant the story in the direction of this or any of the other topics below. In overheard conversations the teacher can take a role to focus discussion on one of the themes.

The Past: In addition to the above students can be given post drama tasks which focus on looking into the past. This could take any form which links to what the students are required to do in the set book. For example, it could bring in information about the past given in the book by asking students how they think their characters in the drama would fit into the world described in the book- verbally or via the post session drama tasks; require students to write about their grandparents' past and compare it to that of the person in the drama; the drama tasks signing the space and time line could both be done with a view to exploring the past rather than the person, etc).

Age: The teacher would maintain the focus on age and perhaps compare the reactions of different ages to different events in the drama.

Describing People and Places: Description would be encouraged both within the session and in post-drama work, verbally and written.

You will also find that general topics such as the Daily News can be introduced into any template by, for example, introducing a newspaper article into the drama, soliciting the writing of a news report of the events of the drama session, or having students make a dramatic presentation of the TV News.

However the most obvious links of topics and templates are those shown in the following table:

Template	Topic
Shopping	Shopping, money, can be adapted for food
Memories	The past, "things ain't what they used to be," people places and things.
Old Age	Age, the past, parents and children
Building On- Minute Stories	Narrative, etiquette
Nursery Rhymes	Fear, morals, prejudice
The Lion's Den	Animal world
Abstract Art	Depends on picture chosen, so could be linked to countless themes
Dramatic approaches to Story	Narrative
Communication is the Key	Communication
Trapped behind enemy lines	War
My Grandfather	Family, the past, age
Emigration	Emigration, geography
Quest	Travel, literature, narrative
Weather	Weather, the seasons; the climate, the environment, the media
Missing Persons	Law and Order; crime
There are Two Sides...	Morals, prejudice
Cinderella	Cultural difference
Delta X	Drugs, health, medicine, the media
The Sibyl	Fame, fortune, power; equality of opportunity

BIBLIOGRAPHY

8. I DRAMA IN THE CLASSROOM

Booth, D. (1984). *Classroom Voices.* Toronto: Harcourt Brace.
Booth, D. (1994). *Storydrama.* Markham: Pembroke Publishers.
Booth, D. & Lundy, C. (1985). *Improvisation.* Don Mills: Academic Press Canada.
Blecher, S, & Jafee, K. (1998). *Weaving in the Arts: Widening the Learning Circle.* Portsmouth: Heinemann.
Cornett, C. (1999). *The Arts as Meaning Makers.* New Jersey: Prentice Hall.
Heller, P.G. (1995). *Drama as a Way of Knowing.* Los Angeles, The Galef Institute.
McCaslin, N. (1990). *Creative Drama in the Classroom.* Studio City, CA: Players Press.
Morgan, N & Saxton, J. (1987). *Teaching Drama.* Cheltenham: Stanley Thornes (Publishers) Ltd.
Morgan, N. & Saxton, J. (1994). *Asking Better Questions.* Markhan Ontario: Pembroke Publishers.
O'Toole, J. (1992). *The Process of Drama.* London: Routledge
Jonstone, R. (1981). *IMPRO: Improvisation and the Theatre.* London: Eyre: Methuen.
Robbie (1995) *A Script for Written Competence: Learning about Writing through Drama* in Warren B (1995)
Stewig, J. (1995). *Language in the Early Childhood Classroom.* Belmont, CA: Wadsworth Publishing Company.
Tarlington, C. (1995). *Building Plays. Simple Playbuilding Techniques at Work.* Portsmouth, NH: Heinemann.
Tarlington, C., & Verriour, P. (1991). *Role Drama.* Portsmouth, NH: Heinemann.
Verriour, P. (1994). *In Role: Teaching and Learning Dramatically.* Markham: Pippin Publishing Limited.
Wagner, B.J. (1998). *Educational Drama and Language Arts: What Research Shows.* Roosevelt University, Chicago, Illinois: Heinemann.
Warren, B. (Ed) (1995). *Creating A Theatre in Your Classroom.* North York, Ontario: Captus Press.

8.2 STORYTELLING

Barton, B & Booth, D. (1990). *Stories in the classroom: Storytelling, Reading Aloud and Role-Playing with children.* Portsmouth, NH: Heinemann.

8.3 GAMES/ACTIVITIES SOURCES

Boal, A. (1992). *Games for Actors and Non-Actors.* London: Routlege.

Booth, D. (1986). *Games for Everyone.* Markham, Ontario: Pembroke Publishers.

Brandes, D. (1982). *Gamester's Handbook.* London: Hutchinson.

Brandes, D. & Phillips, H. (1979). *Gamesters' Handbook: 140 Games for Teachers and Group Leaders.* Cheltenham, England: Stanley Thornes.

Erin, P. & Lewis J. C. (Illustrator) (1996). *Drama in the Classroom: Creative Activities for Teachers, Parents & Friends.* Lost Coast Press.

Green, H. & Gellespie Martin, S. (1981). *Sprouts: Projects for Creative Growth in Children.* Carthage, IL: Good Apple.

Maley A. & Duff, A. (1978). *Variations on a Theme: resource material for listening comprehension and fluency practice.* Cambridge: Cambridge University Press. (Has good material/scenarios easily adapted into a drama setting.)

Maley, A. & Duff, A. (1982; 2nd Ed). *Drama Techniques for Language Learning: a resource book of communication activities for language teachers.* Cambridge: Cambridge University Press.

Patterson, D. & Leveson, M. (1989). *Whose Line is it Anyway?* London: Century Hutchinson Ltd.

Rinvolucri M. (1985). *Grammar Games: Cognitive, Affective and Drama Activities for ESL Students.* Cambridge: Cambridge University Press.

Rinvolucri M. & Davis P. (1996). *More Grammar Games: Cognitive, Affective and Movement Activities for EFL Students.* Cambridge: Cambridge University Press.

Scher, A. & Verral, C. (1975). *100+ Ideas for Drama.* London: Heinemann.

Scher, A. & Verral, C. (1975). *Another 100+ Ideas For Drama 2nd ed.* London: Heinemann.

Warren, B. (1996, 2nd Ed). *Drama Games: Drama and Group Activities for Leaders Working with People of all Ages and Abilities.* North York, Canada: Captus Press.

Wilhelm, J. & Edmiston, B. (1998). *Imagining to Learn. Inquiry, Ethics, and Integration Through Drama.* Portsmouth, NH: Heinemann.

8.4 DRAMA STRUCTURES

Clark, J. & Dobson, W. & Goode, T. & Neelands, J. 1997). *Lessons For The Living.* New Market, Ontario: Mayfair Cornerstone Limited.

Neelands, J. (1990). *Structuring Drama Work.* Cambridge: Cambridge University Press.

Swartz, L. (1995). *Drama Themes.* Ontario, Canada: Pembroke Publishers.

8.5 GROUP FORMATION AND PRE-REHEARSAL EXERCISES

Booth, D. & Lundy, C. (1985). *Improvisation.* Don Mills: Academic Press Canada.

Jennings, S. (1986). *Creative Drama in Groupwork.* Bicester, Oxon, UK: Winslow Press.

Maley, A & Duff, A. (1982; 2nd Ed). *Drama Techniques for Language Learning: a resource book of communication activities for language teachers.* Cambridge: Cambridge University Press.

Swartz, L. (1995). *Drama Themes.* Ontario, Canada: Pembroke Publishers.

8.6 POETRY SOURCES

Booth, D. & Moore, B. (Eds). (1988). *Poems Please: Sharing Poetry with Children.*
Booth, D. (1990). *Voices on the Wind.* Toronto, Canada: Kids Can Press.
Camerion, B. Hogan, M. & Lashinar, P. (1983). *Poetry in Focus.* Toronto: Globe/ Modern Curriculum Press.
Carle, E. (1988). *Eric Carle's Treasury Of Classic Stories For Children.* New York: Scholastic Inc.
Ferris, H. (Ed.) (1957). *Favorite Poems, Old and New.* New York: Doubleday & Company.
Harrison, M. & Stuart-Clark, C. (1990). *The Oxford Book of Story Poems.* Oxford: Oxford University Press.
Lee, D. (1977). *Garbage Delight.* Toronto: Gage Publishing Co.
Morgan, G. & Routley, C.B. (Eds) (1964). *Poems for Boys and Girls, Book One.* Vancouver, Canada: Copp Clark Co.
Patten, B. (Ed.) (1991). *The Puffin Book of Twentieth-Century Children's Verse.* New York: Penguin Books.
Silverstein, S. (1974). *Where the Sidewalk Ends.* New York: Harper & Row Publishers.
Silverstein, S. (1981). *A Light in the Attic.* New York: Harper & Row Publishers.

8.7 IMAGE/PICTURE AND ART WORK

King, N. (1993). *Storymaking and Drama.* USA: Heinemann.
Micklethwait, L. (selected by) (1996). *A Child's Book of Play in ART.* London: Dorling Kindersley Limited.
Montgomery, M., E. (1989). *Norman Rockwell.* New York: Gallery Books.
Van Allsburg, C. (1996). *The Mysteries of Harris Burdick (Portfolio Edition).* Boston: Houghton Mifflin.
Whitin, P. (1996). *Stretching Stories, Stretching Minds: Responding visually to Literature.* Portsmouth: Heinemann.
Yerka, J. (1994). *The Fantastic Art of Jacek Yerka.* Beverly Hills California: Morpheus International.

8.8 CINDERELLA BOOKS

Bell, A. (translated). (1999). *Cinderella. A Fairy Tale by Charles Perrault.* London: North-shore Books.
Egan Betts, L. (retold). (1990). *The Classic Grimm's Fairy Tales.* Philadelphia: Courage Books.
Climo, S., & Heller, R. (1989). *The Egyptian Cinderella.* New York: Harper Collins Publishers.
ISBN 0-06443279-3
Climo, S., & Heller, R. (1993). *The Korean Cinderella.* Mexico: Harper Collins Publishers.
ISBN 0-06-443397-8
Climo, S., & Florczak, R. (1999). *The Persian Cinderella.* USA: Harper Collins Publishers.
ISBN 0-06-026763-1
Climo, S., & Krupinski, L. (1996). *The Irish Cinderlad.* USA: Harper Collins Publishers.
ISBN 0-06-024396-1

LingLouie, A., & Young, E. (1982) *Yeh-Shen.* New York: The Putnam & Grosset Group.
ISBN 0-698-11388-8

Lum, D., & Nagano, M. (1994). *The Golden Slipper.* USA: Troll Associates Inc.
ISBN 0-8167-3406-2

Martin, R., & Shannon, D. (1992). *The Rough-Face Girl.* New York: The Putnam & Grosset Group.
ISBN 0-698-11626-7

Mayer, M., & Craft, K. (1994). *Baba Yaga and Vasilisa the Brave.* New York: Morrow Junior Books.
ISBN 0-688-08500-8

Mehta, L., & Chhaniara, N. (1985). *The Enchanted Anklet.* Toronto, Ontario: Lilmur Publishing.
ISBN 0-9692729-0-1

And many more.

8.9 RELATED ARTICLES AND RESEARCH

Barrs, M. (1987). "Voice and Role in Reading and Writing." *Language Arts* 64: 2: 207-218

Franks, A. (1995). "The Body as a Form of Representation." *Social Semiotics,* 5 (1): 1-121

Robbie, S. (1998). "Drama and Writing in the English as a Foreign Language Classroom." *An Experimental Study of the Use of Drama to Promote Writing in the Foreign Language Classroom.* PhD., Institute of Education, University of London.

Robbie, S. & Warren, B. (1996). "Taoist Approaches to the Shakespearean Sonnet: An Examination of an Innovative Approach to Teaching Verse to Non Native Speakers of English." *Research in Drama in Education* 1 (2), 233-243.

Wagner, BJ. (1998). "Educational Drama and Language Arts: What Research Shows." Portsmouth: Heinemann.

Wagner, B.J. (1994) "Drama and Writing." In Alan Purvis, ed. *The Encyclopaedia of English Studies and Language Arts,* vol. 1, 403-405.

Wagner, BJ. (1983). "The Expanding Circle of Informal Classroom Drama. In Beverly A. Busching and Schwartz, J.I. eds., Integrating the Language Arts in the Elementary School, 155-163. Urbana, IL: National Council of Teachers of English.

Wilkinson, J. A. (1992). "Review of Research on the Relationship between Symbolic Dramatic Play and Literacy." In Wilkinson, J.A., ed., *International Drama Education Research.* Detroit: NARA

Yaffe, S. H. (1989). "Drama as a teaching tool." *Educational Leadership.* 46: 29-32.

8.10 MUSIC SOURCES

"Four Seasons", A. Vivaldi *In the Hall of the Mountain Kings,* E. Grieg
"Carnival of the Animals", Camille Saint-Saens
"The Sorcerer's Apprentice", Disney
"The Pastoral Symphony", No. 6, L. van Beethoven
"Rite of Spring", Igor Travinsky
"Fantasia", Disney
"The Lion King", Disney

APPENDICES

9. I ABSTRACT ART

GUIDED IMAGERY

Note: teachers should read this script slowly and pause regularly so that visual images can form in the minds of students.

- Close your eyes, imagine the setting from the picture is now before you.
- Take a step forward into the setting. Take some time to look around you.
- If this is your first time here, you may find the surroundings new and rather strange. If you have been here before you may have certain feelings about this place.
- As you look about, what do you see? Are you surprised by what you see, or have you seen this before?
- Do certain smells fill the space you are in?
- What are those smells? Are they pleasant? Do they remind you of anything or do they make you think of anything. Do the smells remind you of anything you may have tasted before?
- What is the temperature like in your space?
- Do you dare touch anything in your space, if so what is it that you would touch what does it feel like?
- How does this space make you feel. Would you come back? Think about why or why not?
- Think about who you are, and why you have come here or why you have come back.

9.2 MY GRANDFATHER

Telling of the Tale

My Grandfather was born in 1901 in a part of Czarist Russia we now call the Ukraine. He spoke Yiddish. He lived with his parents on a farm with his two older brothers and two younger sisters. The family worked the land and were satisfied with their life UNTIL the persecutions/pogroms began

My Grandfather was only three years old when the family had to leave in 1904. They could only take with them what they were able to carry. They journeyed over land for two long years until finally, late in 1906, they arrived in the East End of London. In those times it was very difficult to be Jewish, living in this area. My Grandfather was forced to work in the markets selling bread.

After a while my Grandfather's father was able to buy a farm in the country, but things did not go well. He was not able to get used to the British way of life, never learned English and began to drink heavily. Eventually, in 1936 he died.

My Grandfather, however, worked very hard and eventually became a successful doctor.

9.3 WEATHER

Music sources

We would suggest any of the following:
- Vivaldi, *Four Seasons*
- Stravinsky, *Rite of Spring*
- Berlioz, *Symphony Fantastique*
- Beethoven, *No. 6.*

Literature link

We suggest any of the following:
- "Go Wind" (Lilian Moore) and "Rain Sizes" (John Ciardi), both in Booth (1990);
- "Snow and Snow" (Ted Hughes) and "Leaves" (Ted Hughes) in Patten, B (Ed.) (1991);
- "Who Likes the Rain?" (Clara Doty Bates), in Morgan, Routley, C.B. (Eds) (1964);
- "Weather is Full of the Nicest Sounds" (Aileen Fischer) in Booth, D and Moore, B (Eds.) (1988) *Poems Please: Sharing Poetry with Children.*

See our bibliography for other sources.

9.4 DRAMATIC EXPLORATION OF STORY

A list of the Cinderella books we have used can be found in the bibliography. The matrix that follows maps the differences across the versions that we have used.

Title	Setting (Fictional and Real)	Characters *hero **heroine	Tasks and Chores	Magic Symbols	Celebration	Garments	Endings
Cinderella (Grimm) European		*Prince **Cinderella • stepsisters • stepmother • godmother	• mending • cooking • cleaning	• Fairy Godmother	• Ball	• Glass Slipper	• The Prince and Cinderella marry.
The Rough-Face Girl Native North American Tale	Village by the Shore/Lake Ontario, Canada	*invisible being **Rough- Face girl • sister to invisible being • (2) sisters • poor old man	• feed flames of fire (hands arms face scarred and burned)	• The Invisible Being	• to meet the Invisible Being	• large moccasin • necklace from dried reeds and shells • cap dress, and leggings made from birch bark • carved pictures of sun, moon, stars and planets on the dress	• Rough Face Girl bathes in the waters of the lakes. Her skin becomes smooth and her hair grows long again. • Rough Face Girl and the Invisible Being marry.
The Egyptian Cinderella	Somewhere in Egypt	*Pharaoh Amasis **Rhodopis • Master • Egyptian Girls	• wash clothes • gather reeds • mending • cooking	• Falcon	• royal court for all subjects	• red rose slipper	• Pharaoh marries Rhodopis
The Korean Cinderella	Somewhere in Korea	*Magistrate **Pear Blossom • Father • stepmother • stepsister.	• fill water jug • hull rice • weed rice paddies • cook/sew	• giant frog • sparrows • black ox	village fair	• straw sandal	• Magistrate and Pear Blossom marry.

Title	Setting (Fictional and Real)	Characters *hero **heroine	Tasks and Chores	Magic Symbols	Celebration	Garments	Endings
The Golden Slipper Vietnamese Tale	Foothills of Red River	*Prince **Tam • poor rice farmer • stepmother • stepsister	• work in fields • housework	• catfish • rooster • horse	• Autumn Festival	• golden brocade slippers • yellow silk blouse • black trousers	• Tam and Prince marry • Stepmother scolds Tam for not being the owner of the slipper
The Persian Cinderella	Persia: Land of Princes	*Prince Mehrdad **Settareh • father • stepsisters	• no chores as family was wealthy	• small blue jug (pari) • godmother	• No Ruz (New Years)	• diamond anklets • dark red silk dress • golden pendant • turquoise bracelet • scarf to cover head	• Prince and Settareh marry • Stepsisters filled with rage so much that their hearts burst.
The Enchanted Anklet. Tale from India	Town called Cindurnagar	* Prince of Suryanagar **Cinduri • Father • stepmother • stepsister	• fetch water • cook • clean • tend cows/buffalo • sell goods door to door	• white water snake with red jewel. (Godfather)	• Navaratri Festival	• anklets of white gold and diamonds • fine fabrics • precious jewels • rubies	• Prince and Cinduri marry. Stepmother and sisters asleep under a tree. Crushed to death as the tree is struck by lightning.

Title	Setting (Fictional and Real)	Characters *hero **heroine	Tasks and Chores	Magic Symbols	Celebration	Garments	Endings
The Irish Cinderlad	Old times Ireland	*Becan **Princess Finola • (3)step sisters • stepmother	• cow herd boy	• speckled bull	• fight the dragon	• shiny buckled boots • sword • belt	• Princess Finola and Becan marry.
Baba Yaga & Vasilisa the Brave. Russian Tale	Far Edge of Forest	*Tzar **Vasilisa • stepmother • stepsisters • Baba Yaga • old woman	• menial tasks • fetch light from Baba Yaga's house	• plain and simple doll	• wedding	• spun fabric	• Vasilisa and the Tzar marry. • Stepmother and sisters engulfed in flames from burning skull.
Yeh-Shen Tale from China	Somewhere in southern China	*King of T'o Han **Yeh-Shen • ttepsister • stepmother	• heavy and unpleasant chores	• fish with golden eyes • golden slipper	• spring festival	• azure blue gown • cloak of feathers • golden scale-like patterned slippers with soals of gold	• Yeh-Shen marries King • Stepmother and sister remain in cave home and crushed to death by flying stone

9.5 DELTA X

OATH OF SECRECY AND ALLEGIANCE

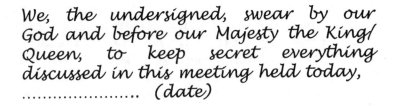

We, the undersigned, swear by our God and before our Majesty the King/Queen, to keep secret everything discussed in this meeting held today, ... (date)

We, the undersigned, hereby swear and sign our names

Top Secret Preliminary Report

TOP   SECRET

It has come to Her Majesty's Government's notice that the drug Deltaxis Demonius, commonly known as Delta X, has been found on the streets. This drug was banned by Her Majesty's Government 10 years ago because of its dangerous effects on health and society.

The drug is reportedly sold in discotheques around the country and is causing many deaths, especially amongst young people. This drug has to be removed from the market again or our whole nation, indeed the whole world is in danger. This message is not to be taken lightly. Delta X has been compared to a nuclear time bomb.

Newspaper article

Hooked on deadly Delta X

Only 14 years of age, hallucinating, unconscious and dehydrated he was found on the pavement outside the Sol and Sombra discotheque last night. It was obvious he had been taking drugs and it did not take long for the doctors at St Mary's to diagnose the deadly Delta X. Four hours later he died in intensive care, before his parents were even known, let alone located.

Yes, Delta X was banned, but it is out on the streets again. And it is out in force. Delta X has been called a "recreational drug". Our special correspondent has been talking to Dr. James Cartwright, consultant at St Mary's Hospital, who finds this name ridiculous. He compares the drug to a plague which is slowly destroying our youth....

REPORTS ON THE DRUG

The teacher should compile documents (one for each group) in accordance with the language level/age of the students on the effects of drugs. These do not need to be very long.

Note these documents can be used to 1) practise structures b) introduce specialist vocabulary (there is evidence that ... etc.).

For example:

Effects on Pregnancy

Studies have associated use of Delta X during pregnancy with lack of growth of the foetus. The decreased weight of the foetus has been related to the amount of Delta X taken. There is also evidence that babies whose mothers take Delta X during pregnancy may have vision problems and shorter attention spans.

9.6 THE SIBYL

The story on the scroll (adapt to language level of students):

Gather round my friends and listen very carefully, I have something to share with you, and I need your help ...

A long time ago, long before the time of Jesus, there was a King called Tarquin who was a ruler of a country far far away from here. We don't know very much about this country except that it was filled with beautiful statues and buildings made from stone. As yet we know very little of Tarquin's people. We know they were extremely clever and we know they carried out rituals. We also know that, being human, they had their problems. In troubled times, in times of hunger or sickness, they journeyed across the mountains to the Cave of the Sibyl. The Sibyl was a prophetess from another country, through whom the Gods of her country spoke. Often she spoke to the people in riddles, prophesizing the future, advising how best to do something.

One day the Sibyl left her cave and came to the Court of King Tarquin. Ceremoniously she put nine scrolls in front of the king and said: "All these will be yours if you give me that which you most value." Tarquin, who was rather afraid of the Sibyl said: "You ask too much. This price is too high."

She then did an extraordinary thing. She burnt three of the scrolls. Then she pointed to the six remaining scrolls and said: "These scrolls will be yours in return for the thing you most value."

Once again King Tarquin refused and the Sibyl burnt three more of the scrolls. By now King Tarquin was anxious to know what these scrolls contained and so he accepted her final offer, three scrolls for the price of the original nine.

The scrolls were locked away and carefully guarded day and night. When they felt they had made the new Gods angry, the guardians of the scrolls would study them for advice as to what should be done. These scrolls became the most valuable thing in Tarquin's kingdom.

That is the end of my story.

GLOSSARY

ARTEFACTS

Tangible objects: an umbrella, a shoe, a box, a hat stand, a doll etc., usually to be used as PROPS.

AUDIENCE INTERVENTION

The audience are either allowed to enter into the drama or to give advice to the characters, usually to help resolve a situation.

AUXILIARY EGO

Class play the conscience of the protagonist, usually by standing behind him and shouting out what his conscience would be saying to him.

BRAINSTORMING

When there are very few set details about a topic, or a topic can be viewed in different ways, the teacher asks questions of the whole class in order to fill in details, or to get different ideas about the same topic.

BUILD BELIEF

It is the teacher's role to BUILD BELIEF, (make the students believe in the drama so that they become rather than act the characters). The more they invest, the better the drama and the better the learning result.

CAPTIONS

Students write a title or caption (hence this is also known as Titles) to a scene or a drama event. This can take the form of a newspaper headline, a song title, etc.

CINQUAIN

A short poem written in 5 lines, as follows:

1st line	one word	topic or title
2nd line	two words	description (adjectives)
3rd line	three words	action (verb)
4th line	four words	feeling/statement about the topic
5th line	one word	synonym for topic/title

i.e., for weather:
wind
tickle, shiver
through my hair
something to giggle about
unexpected

CLOZE

This is a term which refers to an exercise used in the teaching of foreign languages, where a text is selected by the teacher and given to the students with words blanked/missed out (perhaps parts of speech or every third word). Students have to fill in the gaps.

CORRIDOR OF VOICES

This technique is used when a character has to make a difficult decision.

One participant takes the role of the character, the other participants form a corridor with their bodies, a long line of pairs facing each other. Let us presume for the example that the character has to decide whether to take a year out of university or to continue studying. One side of the corridor are in favour of going away for a year, one side are against.

Participants should be fairly spaced out. Lights should be dimmed. It is important for the character to enter role and be focussed. When done with conviction this exercise can be very powerful.

The character steps forward and walks very slowly through the corridor of voices. As the character passes each person the person either shouts, whispers or says their argument: stay and work, you will finish earlier, get it over and done with, you'll miss your friends/ go and be free, you deserve a break, you can do it later, think of the guys on the beach ... etc.

This is sometimes followed by the character retracing his steps and the participants shouting out yes/no/yes/no/yes/no...

The character then has the responsibility of making the decision — yes or no.

Adaptations:

- The participants in the corridor take up positions (physically) as a character who could advise the protagonist (his mother, his teacher, his colleague, etc.) and advise in role, with action. e.g. mother wagging finger: I have sacrificed so much for you to study, etc.

- The corridor emulates the crossroads in the character's life, turning off in a different direction half way or even taking the shape of a cross. Instead of one side of the corridor being for and one against, one half of the corridor is FOR and the other half AGAINST.

CREATING A STORYLINE

Students build a story from a stimulus — a story, an artefact, a picture, etc.

A DAY IN THE LIFE

Through a series of scenes or tableaux, the groups present different things that happened to the same character during 24 hours, for example morning, noon and evening. As the scenes progress, information learned in the previous scene is taken into consideration. The aim is to fill in more about the character. This is often used to find out what happened 24 hours prior to a key moment in the drama.

DISCUSSION IN GROUPS

Students discuss in groups before sharing findings with the class as a whole.

DRAMA

Drama as used in this book is drama used for educational purposes, as a medium within which to work.

DRAMA CIRCLE

When participants are not in role, when discussions and decisions are made, they often sit (on the floor) in a circle, called the drama circle. In the circle they speak as students and the teacher as teacher. Out of the circle they are either part of a drama or working on a drama.

DRAMA SESSION

This is a period of non-stop drama work, following a theme, as exemplified in our templates. It could also be called a lesson or a workshop.

DRAMATIZED SYNOPSIS

A summary, or the main points of the story, told through drama.

ELEMENTS OF STORY

The basic elements of story are:

Given Circumstances:
- character (who?)
- setting/ place (where?)
- time (when?)

Storyline
- plot (what?)
- action (how?)
- purpose (why?)

Almost all stories have a beginning, middle and end. They follow the basic pattern of:
1. established given circumstances
2. developing storyline(s)
3. resolving entanglements and conflicts presented in the story.

FORUM THEATRE

Whilst a group plays out a scene, a member from the audience can shout STOP. The actors freeze. The member of the audience then places a hand on one of the characters in the scene, who withdraws. The member of the audience then takes the place of the character who has withdrawn. This can happen many times during a scene. The aim is to move the drama on, or to develop focus if it loses direction.

FREEZE

Stop all action, stop all motion and stand still!

GIVING WITNESS

A character speaks directly to the audience or in monologue in order to present their side of a case. The case presented is always highly subjective.

GROUP FORMATION EXERCISES

Different fun exercises to get the class into random size groups.

GROUP IMPROVISATION

This is when a group, usually the whole class, works together in some improvised activity. See improvisation.

GUIDED IMAGERY

Guided imagery gives students the opportunity to create a visual picture in their minds as the teacher stimulates their imagination through vivid description or by prompting questions or statements.

Students can be lying on the floor or sitting comfortably with their eyes closed. The idea is to transport the student to another place or time. It is helpful for the inexperienced teacher to prepare a script for the guided imagery ahead of time. With practice, this can be improvised. Some teachers like to play atmospheric music in the background.

For example:

If a picture is used (see Abstract Art template): *Take a step into the picture and carefully look around. What do you see? (short pause) What do you hear? (short pause) Can you smell, taste anything? ... What can you touch? ... How do you feel? ... What memories come to mind ... What are you reminded of?*

If a story is being built from music or pure imagination: *You are flying above the mountains in a small plane, what time of year is it? ... what time of day is it? ... how do you feel? ... look below out of the window: what can you see? ... what colours can you see?.....do you like what you see?*

Note: Teachers should read the script slowly and pause regularly so that visual images can form in the minds of students.

HOTSEAT

This technique is used to find out more about a character or to move the drama forward. It usually works better if the lights are dimmed.

We have devised our own form of hotseating, for language students. The idea is not to put any one student on the spot by question/answer, unless they decide to take the hotseat themselves. We use the hotseat in stages, but teachers can decide to use all or only one of the stages.

Our Adaptation

Participants form a circle and a chair (the hotseat) is placed in the centre of the circle. We usually start by leaving the hotseat free and substituting a visual image which symbolizes the character the group wish to question, or find out more about. (E.g., a crown indicates the king, a duster indicates the maid, a lipstick indicates the wife.)

Anyone in the circle can ask questions of the hotseat. Anyone in the circle, in role, can answer. For example someone asks: "How old are you?" Someone else answers "I'm 22." The idea is that the class as a group ask questions and accept group responsibility for the answers. The idea is to answer in character to build the character. The character may or may not wish to answer all of the questions.

Participants are not singled out when they speak, they take it in turns to speak and other participants look at the chair rather than the person who is speaking.

Original Version

The next (original) stage is for someone from the circle to take the place on the hotseat and, in role, answer the questions asked of them. This person then has the responsibility of building the role as the rest of the class ask the questions. As before, the character may or may not wish to answer all of the questions.

Further Adaptations

Teachers can make up their own modifications of this exercise:

a) the character on the hotseat is not there but merely symbolized and the participants in the circle are people who know something about the person in the centre — for example they are courtiers who know a lot about the king, and take it in turn to divulge information about him. He locks himself up in his chambers for hours every evening. Strange people have been coming into the palace. He has a secret lover.

b) The visual image of the character is passed around the circle and when a participant gets the article they have to answer the next question as if they were on the hotseat.

IMMERSION

Students are immersed in a language which is not their own, the target language (TL) in which they are taught some or all of their classes.

IMPROVISATION

Drama action without using a script, without having worked out what will be said and in many cases what will happen. Participants have to think on their feet: the character makes up the words as he goes along and/or the scene develops as it unrolls. See also **GROUP IMPROVISATION**.

IN ROLE

Working in role means that the person in question assumes the character of someone in the drama and remains faithful to that role. From this come the expressions **Teacher in Role** and **Student in Role**. When the teacher is in role she does not speak as the teacher but as the character.

For language teachers doing role dramas for the first time it may be useful to establish the norms of when a teacher is in or out of role. It could be the teacher uses a prop (object of clothing or something she holds) or stands in a part of the room or uses a different voice to indicate she is in role.

IN ROLE DRAMA

This refers to the assumption of a character, a role, by the participants. The drama is then carried out in role. The participants are literally to become the characters rather than act them.

INTERVIEWS

Carried out in pairs. Instead of having separate pairs working in different parts of the classroom have the students form two circles, one facing inwards and one outwards, so that everyone is facing someone. Make one circle the interviewers and the other the interviewees. Give students a set period of time to interview their pair, then clap your hands and students have to move two paces to the right. then they have another set period of time to interview someone else. The teacher can later reverse the roles so that interviewers become interviewees and vice versa.

IN THE MANNER OF THE WORD

This is an exercise that concentrates on adverbs. Students are asked to do things and are given a certain adverb which they have to link to their action (clean the window slowly or clumsily, answer the telephone excitedly, noisily, abruptly). This could also refer to a whole drama scene, i.e., the interview has to be carried out in the manner of the word ... aggressively, timidly, etc.

IN THE STYLE OF

Drama action is carried out in a well know style, such as a spaghetti western, a melodrama, a comedy, a soap opera, a Shakespearean play, T.V. news report, pop video etc.

LANGUAGE ABILITIES

Different language abilities which are practised through carrying out the drama. See sections 7.1 and 7.2.

LIGHTS

Lighting is important in a drama setting. Often dimming or turning up the lights or closing the curtains/blinds can make a difference to the atmosphere of the drama and the concentration of the participants.

MANTLE OF THE EXPERT

A drama situation is created in which the students assume the roles of experts of some kind, for example they imagine they are all archaeologists or scientists, endowed with special knowledge. They act as if they are experts. These characters will be given a special task to accomplish, for which they need their specialist knowledge.

MIME

Movement/acting without speech.

MONTAGE

Showing both sides of a question at the same time by juxtaposing form and content. For example one group mimes a scene where a friend visits a happy family household whilst another group, simultaneously, provides the dialogue that had taken place prior to the visit when the household was in turmoil.

OVERHEARD CONVERSATIONS

Literally conversations which are overheard by the audience, which the character does not mean anyone else to hear.

PUZZLE POETRY

Write out words and endings of words on pieces of paper or cards which can then be spread on the floor, collected and assembled (placed together) to form pieces of prose or poetry.

PHOTOGRAPH

Students compose a photograph using their bodies, (taking the place of the people/things in the photograph). This photography is formed of a still image/tableau.

PRE-DRAMA ACTIVITIES

Games and activities used as a warm up, to get students moving and/or speaking before a drama session.

PROPS

Articles used in the drama, such as a hat or a book.

RITUAL

The carrying out of a ceremony (usually where things are repeated) or the traditional following of a set of rules. Often particular to a certain cultural or ethnic group.

ROLE REVERSAL

Either: Participants change roles. If Mary were the victim and Joe the policeman, Mary becomes the policeman and Joe the victim.

Or: The policemen act out the way they think the victims feel and the victims act out the way they think the policemen feel.

SCRIBE

Someone writes things down for the rest of the class (if a character is being built, things the class finds out about him are recorded on the board by a member of the class).

SIGNING THE SPACE

The recreation of a space important to a character in the drama. This usually involves the production of written materials. For example a character's office could be recreated, where his diary, his shopping list, his calendar, his letters and his books are all to be found. Participants write these out whilst physically recreating the space. Usually the teacher then requires a scene to take place in that space. The aim is to create the space in keeping with the character whilst also finding out something new about him and to solicit different types of writing.

SILENT MOVIE

A film without words. Participants act out the story without words.

SOUND

This can refer to any means of making sound — musical instruments, music on CDs, or tapes, sounds made with the voice, hands or feet or other soundmakers.

SOUNDMAKERS

Instruments (which may be known musical instruments, hand-made instruments, voices, hands or feet or body parts) which are used to make sounds in a Soundscape.

SOUNDSCAPE

In a soundscape (also called soundtracking) students use soundmakers to create a collage of sound. This collage of sound usually creates mood or tells a story. It can be combined with dialogue to enhance a scene.

SPACE

It is important to ensure good use of space. Monitor groups to make sure everyone can see and everyone can hear. If the rest of the class cannot hear they will lose interest.

STATUES

Students form statues with their bodies.

STILL IMAGE

See tableau.

STORYBUILDING

Creating a story by establishing the elements of story and elaborating around them.

STORYDRAMA

Storydramas take a story as a base. The story could be something that has happened to one of the participants or part of a film or play they have seen. When creating a story drama what is important is that the tale has a sense of person, place, time and purpose. However it should leave OUT details so that a range of possibilities come into play.

STUDENT IN ROLE (SIR)

See in role.

SUSPEND DISBELIEF

This term relates to the commitment of the students to the task. Students have to believe in what they are doing and enter the drama, adopting rather than playing the roles in question. If their treatment of the subject is superficial this can result in giggles and lack of commitment to the task. Should this happen at any time, the teacher should stop the drama action and start again.

TABLEAU

A tableau (also called a still image) is a frozen, still shot of a scene, often one which is particularly vivid or representative. Participants take the place of the characters, using their bodies to convey the moment through a concrete image. This can also take the form of a photograph.

Teacher may later ask participants to develop this into a mime or improvisation.

TARGET LANGUAGE (TL)

The language which the student is studying, be it their mother tongue or second third or fourth language and whether or not it is part of their immediate surroundings.

TEACHER IN ROLE (TIR)

See in role.

THOUGHT TRACKING

This is usually used with tableaux. The teacher or a member of the audience places a hand on a character and asks the character a question. The character will then reply. (what are you feeling right now?).

TIME LINE

Class is divided into groups. Each group decides upon an age during the life of a character. Each group presents an important moment in the person's life, which tells us something about the character. The ages should be sufficiently apart so as not to clash. Each scene should take into account those that have gone before to keep the storyline consistent, so students also have to adapt their scene to what has gone before.

VISUAL SOURCES

Things that can been seen, such as pictures, drawings, paintings, used as stimuli for dramas. These sources should include some or all of the following elements:
- show events that suggest dramatic elements;
- portray interesting characters;
- possess intriguing qualities;
- express subtle messages;
- offer possibility for subjective work;
- present ambiguity;
- express tension or a problem;
- promote thought;
- stimulate reflection;
- make use of contrasting elements: dark/light; cold/warm; loud/quiet; hard/soft etc.

VOICES IN THE HEAD

This technique is similar to the corridor of voices, also used when a character has to make a difficult decision, not necessarily a yes/no. For example it could be how they are to deal with another person or situation. The class become the character's inner conscience.

One way to do this is for two characters that represent opposing views on the subject to sit facing one another on the floor. If the protagonist is not one of these (s)he should watch the session. The rest of the class sit behind the person whose viewpoint they take. In turns people behind the characters speak aloud as if they are the character's alter ego. The characters themselves do not speak, only listen.

When the teacher terminates the session the characters now speak and the protagonist makes his decision.
This is also sometimes called Auxiliary Ego

WEB

A pictorial record of a brainstorming session (the word to be brainstormed is written in the middle and the other words associated with it are written around it, either singly or in clusters of like associated words). The teacher will circle the word in the centre and draw lines out to the other words resulting from the brainstorming. Thus the pictorial record forms a sort of spider's web.

INDEX

PROPERTY OF
Baker College Allen Park